NUT**SHELLS**

International Law

D1081033

YOU'VE GOT IT CRACKED

Nutcases – your essential revision and starter guides

- Provides you with in-depth case analysis of the facts, principles and decision of the most important cases in an area of law

- Incorporates colour to help distinguish cases and legislation and aid ease of use

- Presents the text in bite-size chunks and includes bullets where appropriate to aid navigation, assimilation and retention of information

- Breaks the subject down into key topics to enable you to easily identify and concentrate on particular topics

- Opens each chapter with a short introduction to outline the key concepts covered and condense complex and important information

- Highlights Court of Appeal and House of Lords cases to enable you to easily identify the relative significance of the cases examined

- Includes boxed "think points" at the end of each chapter providing further case analysis

- Fully indexed by individual cases and topics

Available from all good booksellers

NUT**SHELLS**

International Law

SECOND EDITION

by
PROFESSOR REBECCA WALLACE
Centre for Rural Childhood, Perth College UHI

ANNE HOLLIDAY
Research Fellow,
Centre for Rural Childhood, Perth College UHI

With research assistance from
FRASER JANECZKO and
KAREN WYLIE

SWEET & MAXWELL  THOMSON REUTERS

First Edition – 2006

Published in 2010 by Thomson Reuters (Legal) Limited
(Registered in England & Wales, Company No 1679046.
Registered Office and address for service:
.   100 Avenue Road, London NW3 3PF)
trading as Sweet & Maxwell

*For further information on our products and services, visit
www.sweetandmaxwell.co.uk*

Typeset by YHT Ltd
Printed in Great Britain by Ashford Colour Press, Gosport, Hants

*No natural forests were destroyed to make this product;
only farmed timber was used and re-planted.*

A CIP catalogue record for this book is available from the British Library.

ISBN 978-0-414-04175-2

Thomson Reuters and the Thomson Reuters logo are trademarks of Thomson Reuters.
Sweet & Maxwell ® is a registered trademark of Thomson Reuters (Legal) Limited

*Crown copyright material is reproduced with the permission of the Controller
of HMSO and the Queen's Printer for Scotland.*

Contents

v

Using this Book

Welcome to our new look NUTSHELLS revision series. We have revamped and improved the existing design and layout and added new features, according to student feedback.

NEW DETAILED TABLE OF CONTENTS for easy navigation.

REDESIGNED TABLES OF CASES AND LEGISLATION for easy reference.

NEW CHAPTER INTRODUCTIONS to outline
the key concepts covered and condense
complex and important information.

Other Statutory R.

. . . .

NATIONAL MINIMUM WAGE ACT

The National Minimum Wage Act 19
minimum hourly rate of pay for all
State to determine and ame
are set: one

**DEFINITION CHECKPOINTS AND
EXPLANATION OF KEY CASES**
to highlight important information.

gives the right to s.
oduct.

> **DEFINITION CHECKPOINT**
>
> A **product** is defined by s.1(2) as any
> product which is comprised in anoth
> being a component part or raw mater
> provides that a product is **defective** if
> *such as persons generally are entitled*

So the Act is not concerned with the
only where products are unsafe. Wh
require an objective consideration
tions a number of factors
in which

KEY CASE

CARMICHAEL V NATIONAL POW
Mrs Carmichael worked as a gu
required" basis, showing group:
tion. She worked some hours m
wore a company uniform, was s
vehicle, and enjoyed many of th
question for the court to determ'
"umbrella" or "global" emplov
which she worked and the in

Held: (HL) During the
ng her duti

DIAGRAMS, FLOWCHARTS AND OTHER DIAGRAMMATIC REPRESENTATION to clarify and condense complex and important information and break up the text.

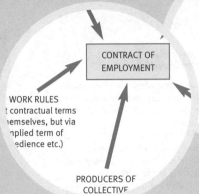

Figure 1 Court and Tribunal System

House of Lords ■ ■ ■ ■

CONTRACT OF EMPLOYMENT

COURT OF APPEAL (CIVIL DIVISION)

WORK RULES
t contractual terms
emselves, but via
nplied term of
edience etc.)

EMPLOYMENT APPEAL TRIBUNAL

PRODUCERS OF COLLECTIVE

END OF CHAPTER REVISION CHECKLISTS outlining what you should now know and understand.

Chapter Checklist

You should now know and underst

- the three heads of claim for
- issues regarding the choice o
- the role of the independent e
- what is meant by "pay".

QUESTION AND AN

END OF CHAPTER QUESTION AND ANSWER SECTION with advice on relating knowledge to examination performance, how to approach the question, how to structure the answer, the pitfalls (and how to avoid them!) and how to get the best marks.

QUESTION AND ANSWER

The Question

David and Emily are employed as machi worked for them for one and a half yea

Emily discovers that David earns £9.0 paid £8.50 per hour. She also disc employed by a subsidiary of XCo ir

HANDY HINTS
– revision and examination tips and
advice relating to the subject features
at the end of the book.

HANDY HINTS

Examination questions in employme
either essay questions or problem que
format and in what is required of the ex
of question in turn.

Students usually prefer one type
normally opting for the problem que
examinations are usually set in a wa
least one of each style of question

Very few, if any, questions
ows about a topic, and it
make a p

NEW COLOUR CODING throughout to
help distinguish cases and legislation
from the narrative. At the first mention,
cases are highlighted in colour and
italicised and legislation is highlighted
in colour and emboldened.

w has d
are an ethnic group (Se
ypsies are an ethnic group (CRE
Rastafarians are not an ethnic group
ment [1993] I.R.L.R. 284)

(d) Jehovah's Witnesses are not an ethnic o
Norwich City College case 1502237/97)

(e) RRA covers the Welsh (*Gwynedd CC v Jone*

(f) Both the Scots and the English are covere
"national origins" but not by "ethnic or
Board v Power [1997], *Boyce v British Ai*

It should be noted that Sikhs, Jews, Je
ians are also protected on
Equality (Religion or

Table of Cases

xiii

TABLE OF CASES

Table of Treaties, International Documents and National Legislation

Definition of International Law

International law can be defined as a body of rules, which regulate the behaviour of states and other entities in their relations with each other, at any given time. This definition represents a departure from the traditional definition, which reflected the view that states were the only subjects of international law. What is required of other entities to participate on the international stage is that they be recognised as possessing some degree of international personality. The primary entities referred to are international organisations and individuals, as well as other non-state actors.

The contemporary definition of international law is open-ended. This is necessary in order to acknowledge that international actors other than states operate on the international plane. The traditional definition was not so accommodating. Historically international law was those rules governing the relations of sovereign states in times of peace and war. However, as the content of international law expanded, such a definition proved to be insufficiently flexible as it failed to take account of the emergence on the international scene of entities such as organisations and individuals. Nevertheless, states remain the primary participants on the international stage.

International law in this context is public international law and is different from private international law—more correctly defined as "conflict of laws"—and foreign relations law.

The History and Development of International Law

International law is of relatively recent origin. It developed because states need to co-exist and because it was simultaneously necessary to establish the limits of state action.

The earliest expressions of international law were the rules of war and diplomatic relations. However the subject matter of international law today covers a wide range of topics—states are in greater contact with each other, issues of international concern demand co-operation and domestic matters are now subject to external review. The international community is no longer a western, European club of 51 states but is now made up of 192 states reflecting different cultural, political and social ideologies.

Contemporary international law has its roots in the sixteenth and seventeenth centuries and its development coincided with the rise of the secular sovereign state in Western Europe. The development of international law mirrors the extent to which states came into contact with each other. This started with laws of warfare and diplomatic relations. However, the so called "Age of Discovery" and the opening of new trade routes, e.g. to the East and West Indies, saw the need for rules relating to validity of title to territory and the articulation of freedom of the high seas. International law by the nineteenth century was a universal system, at least geographically, although it reflected Western European traditions and values. In other words, although international in application it could not be said to be international in content.

As contact between states became more frequent the subject matter of international law extended and today covers a wide range of topics. There is also growing recognition that certain issues of international concern can only be resolved through collaborative action and co-operation is prerequisite. Furthermore, matters which were previously thought to be exclusively domestic are now regarded as international, e.g. treatment of one's own nationals may be the subject of external review.

Main characteristics of the international legal system vis-à-vis domestic law

International law is often criticised as not being law. It is true that international law cannot be understood in the same way as domestic law.

The international legal system is decentralised and based on consent unlike any domestic legal system, which is centralised and imposed. The role of consent is best reflected in the way in which international law is made: through treaties, which are agreements between consenting states; and customary international law, which has emerged through the practice of states endorsed by consent. There is also provision within the international legal system for "opting out" from the application of treaty provisions or customary international law. Such flexibility is not available within domestic legal systems.

There is no international legislature enacting binding rules nor is there an international executive enforcing international law. There is an International Court of Justice (ICJ) where states can seek a solution to disputes, but acceptance of the ICJ's jurisdiction is again based on consent and is not mandatory. Similarly, acceptance of the permanent International Criminal Court's (ICC) jurisdiction is also based on consent. However, once created, international law assumes a mandatory characteristic and should not be disregarded by those subject to it.

Reciprocity plays an important role in the creation and observance of international law; reciprocity helps to guarantee that states more frequently respect each other's sovereignty. Sanctions are available by way of economic sanctions through the United Nations (UN) and the use of force may be legitimately employed in certain defined circumstances. Also public opinion should not be underestimated as a useful barometer in maintaining respect for international law.

Much of the criticism international law attracts stems from the fact that frequently international law breaks down in areas which are politically sensitive and which accordingly attract wide media coverage. However international law operates very effectively and successfully on a regular day-to-day basis in different sectors, e.g. it is the means whereby international travel and international communications, to name but two, take place.

QUESTION AND ANSWER

The Question

The development of international law is a reflection of the international global community.

Critically discuss.

Advice and the Answer

Initially discuss the origins of international law and identify the major milestones in its development, emphasing that the increasing contact between states necessitated that the parameters of state activity be defined. The "Age of Discovery" required rules for establishing title to territory. All states, in theory, are equal but the weight attached to the view of a state is commensurate with its political standing in the international community. The decentralised structure of the international legal system also reflects the international community within which it operates. The diversity of the international community demands that the international legal system is accommodating and flexible.

Sources of International Law

3

. . . .

INTRODUCTION

The best starting place for determining the sources of international law is art.38(1) of the Statute of the ICJ. Article 38 makes no reference to the term "sources" but is rather a direction to the ICJ on how disputes coming before it should be tackled. Article 38 is regarded as an authoritative statement on sources of international law.

TREATY HIGHLIGHTER

Article 38(1) of the Statute of the ICJ directs the Court to decide disputes referred to it in accordance with international law by applying:

"(a) international conventions, whether general or particular, establishing rules expressly recognised by the contesting States;
(b) international custom, as evidence of a general practice accepted as law;
(c) the general principles of law recognised by civilised nations;
(d) subject to the provisions of Article 59, judicial decisions and the teachings of the most highly qualified publicists of the various nations, as subsidiary means for the determination of the rules of law".

The first three are regarded as formal sources whereas the last is regarded as a material source. Formal sources constitute what the law is whereas material sources state where the law may be found.

No reference is made in art.38 to a hierarchy of procedure. However, it is clear that the article establishes a hierarchy whereby:

Any treaty provision existing between the parties to the dispute must be applied;

If there is no treaty then a rule of international custom should be applied;

If there is neither a prevailing treaty provision nor a custom then general principles are turned to; and

In the absence of any of the foregoing, look to judicial decisions and writings as a subsidiary means for determining the law.

CUSTOM

Customary international law is conduct or behaviour which is engaged in because those doing so feel legally obliged to behave in such a way. It is also felt that failure to follow the custom will incur legal penalties.

Custom is different from "usage", which is behaviour engaged in out of friendship or political expediency.

What distinguishes custom from "usage"?

Custom must possess two elements: a material element and a psychological element.

The material element refers to behaviour of states, in other words, state practice. The psychological element denotes states believing that the conduct is not discretionary but mandatory. *Opinio juris* sive necessitatis is the technical term used to describe the subjective feeling of states that certain conduct is mandatory.

MATERIAL ELEMENT

Criteria for assessment of material element

Duration of state practice—there is no set time limit required. The passage of only a short period of time is not necessarily, of itself, a bar to the formulation of a new rule of customary international law.

NORTH SEA CONTINENTAL SHELF (1969) I.C.J. REP. 3.

These cases involved agreements made between the Federal Republic of Germany (FRG) and the Netherlands in 1964, and FRG and Denmark in 1965. The agreements established partial maritime boundaries in the immediate vicinity of their North Sea coasts. However, further agreement had proved impossible and special agreements were concluded between the respective parties referring the matter to the ICJ. The question posed to the ICJ was:

"What principles and rules of international law are applicable to the delimitation as between the parties of the areas of the Continental Shelf in the North Sea which appertain to each of them beyond the partial boundary as determined?"

The ICJ joined the two cases. Denmark and the Netherlands maintained the appropriate principle for determining the boundary line should be "equidistance-special circumstances principle" as contained in Article 6(2) of the 1958 Geneva Convention on the Continental Shelf. The FRG denied this in favour of "the doctrine of the just and equitable share".

Denmark and the Netherlands were parties to the Continental Shelf Convention whereas FRG, although a signatory, was not a party to it. Denmark and the Netherlands maintained art.6(2) incorporating the equidistance principle reflected customary international law at the time it was adopted.

Regarding "time limit" the ICJ acknowledged:

"Although the passage of only a short period of time is not necessarily, or of itself, a bar to the formation of a new rule of customary international law on the basis of what was originally a purely conventional rule, an indispensable requirement would be that within the period in question, short though it might be, State practice including that of States whose interests are specially affected, should have been both extensive and virtually uniform in the sense of the provision invoked—and should moreover have occurred in such a way as to show a general recognition that a rule of law or legal obligation is involved."

Extent of state practice—state practice must be extensive and virtually uniform—see *North Sea Continental Shelf* cases Key Case (see above) and the *Asylum* case (see below, p.8).

THE ASYLUM CASE (1950) I.C.J. REP. 266.
This case arose between Colombia and Peru when a Peruvian national was granted asylum by Colombia in its Embassy in Lima, Peru. The individual was wanted in Peru following an unsuccessful rebellion in that country. Colombia's request for his safe conduct out of Peru was refused. Colombia then brought the case to the ICJ for a ruling as to whether it—the state granting asylum—was competent to qualify the offence, charged for this purpose, under both treaty and American international law in general or "regional or local custom peculiar to Latin American States." The ICJ emphasised:

"The Party which relies on a custom of this kind must prove that this custom is established in such a manner that it has become binding on the other Party. The Colombian Government must prove that the rule invoked by it is in accordance with a constant and uniform usage practised by the States in question, that this usage is the expression of a right appertaining to the State granting asylum and a duty incumbent on the territorial State. This follows from Article 38 of the Statute of the ICJ, which refers to international custom "as evidence of a general practice accepted as law.""

It should be noted that inconsistency in itself does not prevent a rule from being accepted as customary international law. However, major inconsistencies would constitute an obstacle in the formation of customary international law.

Practice does not require the involvement of all states, but practice has to be accepted as law. Uniformity is higher in respect of regional customs because of the fewer number of states involved, see *Asylum* case (see above).

Identity of states

The identity of those whose interests are specially affected is relevant, see *North Sea Continental Shelf* cases (see above, p.7).

Evidence of state practice

Treaties; diplomatic correspondence; opinions of national/legal advisers; states practice within international organisations; and comments by governments on International Law Commission drafts all indicate state practice.

E.g. with reference to state practice as manifested within international organisations and conferences:

> "it cannot be denied, with regard to the resolutions which emerge therefrom, or better, with regard to the votes expressed therein in the name of States, that these amount to precedents contributing to the formation of custom."

See separate opinion of Judge Ammoun in *Barcelona Traction Light and Power Company* case *(Second Phase)* (1970) I.C.J. Rep. 3.

In the case *Concerning Military and Paramilitary Activities in and Against Nicaragua (Merits)* (1986) I.C.J. Rep. 14, the ICJ relied exclusively on General Assembly Resolutions to demonstrate that *opinio juris* existed in respect of the prohibition on the use of force. In the same case the ICJ noted that statements by high-ranking official political figures could be, "of particular probative value when they acknowledge facts or conduct unfavourable to the State represented by the person who made them." However, the ICJ stated that such statements should be treated with caution.

Overt state practice is important as seen in *Continental Shelf (Libya v. Malta)* (1985) I.C.J. Rep. 13, where the ICJ stated, "it is of course axiomatic that the material of customary international law is to be looked for primarily in the actual practice and *opinio juris* of States."

. . . .

PSYCHOLOGICAL ELEMENT

Opinio juris sive necessitatis
The main difficulty here is establishing the existence of such a psychological element. The burden of proof lies with the state seeking to rely on the custom.

> **KEY CASE:**
>
> **LOTUS CASE (FRANCE V TURKEY) (1927) P.C.I.J. SERIES A NO. 10 18**
> In this case, France failed to demonstrate that non-prosecution by the victim's flag state was done because of a legal obligation to do so. This followed a collision on the high seas between a French vessel—the Lotus—and a Turkish vessel. The latter sank and eight Turkish sailors were lost. On arrival in Constantinople the French Officer on watch on the Lotus was arrested and charged with involuntary manslaughter.
> The question put to the ICJ was whether Turkey in exercising

jurisdiction over the French Officer was acting contrary to international law and in particular to art.15 of the Convention of Lausanne 1923. However, the ICJ held:

"There is no rule of international law in regard to collision cases to the effect that criminal proceedings are exclusively within the jurisdiction of the State whose flag is flown ... The conclusion could only be overcome if it were shown that there was a rule of customary international law, which ... established the exclusive jurisdiction of the States whose flag was flown ... in the Court's opinion, the existence of such a rule has not been conclusively proved."

The ICJ continued:

"Even if the rarity of the judicial decisions to be found ... were sufficient to prove ... the circumstances alleged ... it would merely show that States had often, in practice, abstained from instituting criminal proceedings, and not that they recognised themselves as being obliged to do so; for only if such abstention were based on their being conscious of having a duty to abstain would it be possible to speak of an international custom."

KEY CASE

NORTH SEA CONTINENTAL CASES (SEE ABOVE, P.7)

Here it was held that although adjacent states had employed the principle of equidistance in determining the continental shelf between them there was no evidence this had been done because the states had felt legally obliged to do so. The ICJ expressed the requirement of *opinio juris* in the following way:

" ... two conditions must be fulfilled. Not only must the acts concerned amount to a settled practice, but they must also be such or be carried out in such a way, as to be evidence of a belief that this practice is rendered obligatory by the existence of a rule of law requiring it. The need for such a belief, i.e. the existence of a subjective element, is implicit in the very notion of the *opinio juris sive neccessitatis*. The States concerned must therefore feel that they are conforming to what amounts to a legal obligation. The frequency or even habitual character of the acts is not in

> itself enough. There are many international acts, e.g. in the field of ceremonial and protocol, which are performed almost invariably, but which are motivated only by considerations of courtesy, convenience or treatment, and not by any sense of legal duty."

The difficulty in proving *opinio juris* has contributed to a greater use of treaties as a means of regulating international law.

DISSENT: THE *PERSISTENT OBJECTOR* THEORY

A state can only avoid being bound by customary international law if it expresses dissent from the outset of the formulation of the custom, and subsequently sustains its dissent.

In the *Anglo Norwegian Fisheries case* (1951) I.C.J. Rep. 116, the ICJ acknowledged that:

> "although the ten-mile rule had been adopted by certain States both in their national law and in their treaties and Conventions, and although certain arbitral decisions have applied it as between these States, other States have adopted a different limit. Consequently, the ten-mile rule has not acquired the authority of a general rule of international law. In any event the ten-mile rule would appear to be inapplicable as against Norway in so much as she has always opposed any attempt to apply it to the Norwegian coast."

It should be noted that new states recognised after customary international law is established are bound, regardless of whether the state agrees with the rule or not.

Amendment of customary international law demands inconsistent conduct from the established customary rule. Whether the proposed change is accepted depends on how the change is received by states. If the new rule receives a widespread positive response then the new rule may establish itself as customary international law very quickly. If it meets with a negative or limited response then the existing rule will continue to exist. If states are equally divided between the established rule and the new rule, change may be slow. This means the legality of the new conduct will be uncertain for an interim period.

Instant custom

Instant custom is an anomalous, self-contradictory term used to describe the response of states to a particular set of new circumstances, e.g. doctrine of the continental shelf and the Exclusive Economic Zone (EEZ). It is rare and an exception to the norm.

Conclusion

Custom, although no longer a major source of international law, remains an important influence and treaty provisions are often a reflection of customary international law.

. . . .

TREATIES

Article 38 does not mention the term "treaty" but treaty is the generic term used in international law to refer to a convention, agreement, protocol or exchange of notes.

TREATY HIGHLIGHTER

The *Vienna Convention on the Law of Treaties 1969 (the Vienna Convention), art.2(1)(a)* defines a treaty as:

"an international agreement concluded between States in written form and governed by international law, whether embodied in a single instrument or in two or more related instruments and whatever its particular designation".

This definition only applies to written treaties between states. Treaties can either be bipartite (between two states) or multipartite (between many states). The more common terms are "bilateral" and "multilateral", respectively. The former are sometimes referred to as treaty contracts—"*traite contracts*"—and the latter as law-making treaties—"*traite lois*". While all treaties apply only to states who are party to them, multilateral treaties may be seen as law-making as they potentially have a wider effect.

Oral statements may have some legal consequences. In the *Legal Status of Eastern Greenland* case (1933) P.C.I.J. Series A/B, No 53, the Norwegian Government, by way of an oral statement via the Norwegian Minister of Foreign Affairs—Mr Ihlen—had declared that Norway would not make any difficulties in the settlement of the question of the extension of Danish sovereignty over Greenland. The question before the PCIJ was whether the aforementioned declaration by Mr Ihlen—if not constituting a definitive recognition of Danish sovereignty—constituted an obligation on Norway to refrain from occupying any part of Greenland. The ICJ held the Ihlen Declaration put it beyond all dispute that by the undertaking:

> "Norway is under an obligation to refrain from contesting sovereignty over Greenland as a whole, and a fortiori to refrain from occupying a part of Greenland."

Furthermore, in the *Nuclear Test cases* (Australia v France and New Zealand v France) (1974) I.C.J. Rep. 253, Australia and New Zealand requested a declaration from the ICJ to the effect the carrying out of nuclear tests in the South Pacific by France, was contrary to international law. The cases were withdrawn from the ICJ's list when France declared that no further tests would be carried out after 1974. The ICJ stated, in regard to these French pronouncements:

> "It is well recognised that declarations made by way of unilateral acts, concerning legal or factual situations, may have the effect of creating legal obligations ... Whether a statement is made orally or in writing makes no essential difference, for such statements made in particular circumstances may create commitments in international law, which does not require that they should be couched in written form ... "

Note, oral statements will only have binding effect if that is the obvious intention of the State concerned, see *Frontier Dispute case (Burkina Faso v Mali)* (1985) I.C.J. Rep. 554.

There is also a parallel Convention—the Vienna Convention on the Law of Treaties between States and International Organisations or Between International Organisations—which was adopted in 1986. The provisions of the 1986 Convention closely resemble those of the 1969 Vienna Convention on the Law of Treaties, but it has yet to enter into force.

Treaties represent the most concrete form by which states can record an agreement. Registration of a treaty in accordance with art.102 of the UN Charter allows it to be invoked before an organ of the UN. Article 102 states:

> "(1) Every treaty and every international agreement entered into by any member of the United Nations after the present Charter comes into force shall as soon as possible be registered with the Secretariat and published by it.
> (2) No party to any such treaty or international agreement which

has not been registered in accordance with the provisions of paragraph 1 of this article may invoke that treaty or agreement before any organ of the United Nations."

See also art.80 of the 1969 Vienna Convention on the Law of Treaties, which provides that:

"Treaties shall, after their entry into force, be transmitted to the Secretariat of the United Nations for registration or filing and recording ... and for publication."

The 1969 Vienna Convention on the Law of Treaties regulates the conclusion and entry into force of treaties, treaty interpretation and amendment and modification of treaties as well as their validity, termination and suspension. It is regarded as reflecting, for the most part, customary international law although certain provisions represent progressive development.

The 1969 Vienna Convention's acceptance as codifying customary international law is endorsed by its application to agreements concluded prior to the Convention. For example, in the *Beagle Channel Arbitration* (1978) 17 I.L.M. 632, the 1969 Vienna Convention on the law of Treaties was applied to the 1881 Treaty concluded between Argentina and Chile. Also, in the case *Concerning the Gabcikovo-Nagymaros Project (Hungary/Slovakia)* (1997) I.C.J. 7; 38 I.L.M. 162, the ICJ noted that:

"The Vienna Convention is not directly applicable to the 1977 Treaty—a bilateral agreement between Hungary and Czechoslovakia—in as much as both states ratified that Convention only after the Treaty's conclusion. Consequently only those rules that are declaratory of customary international law are applicable ... "

Article 6 of the 1969 Vienna Convention provides that every state possesses the capacity to conclude treaties. Before a state representative can conclude a treaty on behalf of a state, the representative must possess full powers:

" ... (c) "full powers" means a document emanating from the competent authority of a State designating a person or persons to represent the State for negotiating, adopting or authenticating the text of a treaty, for expressing the consent of the State to be bound by a treaty, or for accomplishing any other act with respect to a treaty; ... "

A state may express its willingness to be bound in one of a number of ways, e.g. signature, ratification. A non-signatory state may accede to the treaty at a later date.

Reservations

A distinctive characteristic of treaties is the possibility for a contracting party to make a reservation to the treaty.

> **TREATY HIGHLIGHTER**
>
> A reservation is defined in art.2(1)(d) of the 1969 Vienna Convention as:
>
> "A unilateral statement, however phrased or named, made by a State, when signing, ratifying, accepting, approving or acceding to a treaty, whereby it purports to exclude or to modify the legal effect of certain provisions of the treaty in their application to that State."

Reservations are only applicable in multilateral treaties. Reservations may be made unless:

some treaties are stricter re reservations than others.

 "(a) the reservation is prohibited by the treaty;
  (b) the treaty provides that only specified reservations, which do not include the reservation in question, may be made; or
  (c) in cases not falling under sub-paragraphs (a) and (b), the reservation is incompatible with the object and purpose of the treaty."—art.19 1969 Vienna Convention.

Reservations must be in writing but a reservation, according to art.20(1), "expressly authorized by a treaty does not require any subsequent acceptance by the other Contracting States unless the treaty so provides."
 However, under art.20(2);

" . . . when it appears from the limited number of the negotiating States and the object and purpose of a treaty that the application of a treaty in its entirety between all the parties is an essential condition of the consent of each one to be bound by the treaty, a reservation requires acceptance by all the parties."

Not only must a reservation be in writing but also an objection and acceptance of such reservation and the reservation must be intimated to all contracting parties. The withdrawal of a reservation or withdrawal of an objection to a reservation must also be formulated in writing, art.23(4).

The effect of a reservation is to modify the reserving state's relations with other state parties. That is with respect to the provisions of the treaty to which the reservation relates, to the extent of the reservation, art.21(1)(a) and (b) "modifies those provisions to the same extent for that other party in its relations with the reserving State". In art.21(2) "the reservation does not modify the provisions of the treaty for the other parties to the treaty *inter se*." Article 21(3) continues:

> "when a State objecting to a reservation has not opposed the entry into force of the treaty between itself and the reserving State, the provisions to which the reservation relates do not apply as between the two States to the extent of the reservation."

Article 22 governs the withdrawal of reservations and provides, for instance, that unless prohibited by the treaty a reservation may be withdrawn at any time.

The *Reservations to the Convention on Genocide* case (1951) I.C.J. Rep. 15 (Advisory Opinion) highlights a flexible approach to reservations. The ICJ gave this Advisory Opinion following a request from the General Assembly on:

1) Whether a reserving State to the Genocide Convention could be regarded as a party to the Convention if some, although not all parties to the Convention objected to the reservation;

2) Given an affirmative answer, what relationship subsisted between the reserving and objecting States as well as the relationship between the reserving State and non-objecting States; and

3) What would be the legal effect of an objection from a signatory State— i.e. a State, which had not yet ratified—or by a State entitled to sign or accede but which had not done so?

The ICJ in its Advisory Opinion and in its response introduced a more flexible approach to reservations, stating, in respect of question one:

> "A State which has made and maintained a reservation which has been objected to by one or more of the parties to the Convention but not by others, can be regarded as being a party to the Convention if the reservation is compatible with the object and purpose of the Convention; otherwise, that State cannot be regarded as being a party to the Convention."

In response to question two:

> "(a) if a party to the Convention objects to a reservation which it considers to be incompatible with the object and purpose of the Convention, it can in fact consider that the reserving State is not a party to the Convention;
>
> (b) if, on the other hand, a party accepts the reservation as being compatible with the object and purpose of the Convention, it can in fact consider that the reserving State is a party to the Convention."

In response to question three, the ICJ stated:

> "(a) that an objection to a reservation made by a signatory State which has not yet ratified the Convention can have the legal effect indicated in the reply to question one only upon ratification. Until that moment it merely serves as a notice to the other State of the eventual attitude of the signatory State;
>
> (b) that an objection to a reservation made by a State which is entitled to sign or accede but which has not yet done so, is without legal effect."

The emphasis is on compatibility with the object and purpose of the treaty, which includes the substantive text and the nature and text of the treaty. The ICJ's opinion is reflected in art.19 of the 1969 Vienna Convention, which in addition to allowing compatible reservations allows reservations provided there is no blanket prohibition or the reservation is of a type specifically excluded.

For an instance of a judicial consideration of object and purpose see the *Restrictions to the Death Penalty* case (1983) 23 I.L.M. 320. In this case, the question before the Inter-American Court of Human Rights was whether the reservation made by Guatemala to art.4 of the American Convention on Human Rights was permissible. Article 4 guarantees the right to life and the reservation by Guatemala was to the effect it did not accept that guarantee prohibiting the use of the death penalty for common crimes relating to political offences which fell under this article. As to the compatibility of such a reservation with the Convention's object and purpose the ICJ concluded the reservation in question was not designed:

> "to deny the right of life as such ... to that extent it can be considered, in principle, as not being incompatible with the object and purpose of the Convention."

Observance and application of treaties

DEFINITION CHECKPOINT
Pacta sunt servanda Article 26 of the 1969 Vienna Convention states, "Every treaty in force is binding upon the parties to it and must be performed by them in good faith."

Treaty interpretation

TREATY HIGHLIGHTER
Articles 31–33 of the 1969 Vienna Convention relate to the interpretation of treaties. Article 31 describes the general rules of interpretation; art.32 describes supplementary means of interpretation, including recourse to preparatory documents; and art.33 describes the rules attaching to treaties authenticated in more than one language.

The general rules of interpretation are set out in art.31:

> "A treaty shall be interpreted in good faith in accordance with the ordinary meaning to be given to the terms of the treaty in their context and in the light of its object and purpose."

This article acknowledges primacy of "ordinary meaning interpretation" but also allows interpretation in accordance with the intention of the parties and the treaty's aims and objectives. The latter, the "teleological approach", is only to assist interpretation.

Article 31(2) deals with the context, for the purposes of interpretation, it includes, in addition to the text, the treaty's preamble and annexes as well as:

> "(a) any agreement relating to the treaty which was made between all the parties in connection with the conclusion of the treaty;
> (b) any instrument which was made by one or more parties in connection with the conclusion of the treaty and accepted by the other parties as an instrument related to the treaty."

In addition account may be taken of any subsequent agreement or practice as to the interpretation of the treaty or the application of its provisions as well as any relevant rules of international law applicable in the relations between the parties, art.31(3). Article 31(4) provides, "a special meaning shall be given to a term if it established that the parties so intended."

Article 32 then provides:

> "Recourse may be had to supplementary means of interpretation, including the preparatory work of the treaty and the circumstances of its conclusion, in order to confirm the meaning resulting from the application of Article 31, or to determine the meaning when the interpretation according to Article 31:
> (a) leaves the meaning ambiguous or obscure; or
> (b) leads to a result which is manifestly absurd or unreasonable."

Third states

DEFINITION CHECKPOINT
Pacta tertiis nec nocent nec prosunt   This is the principle that third parties receive neither rights nor duties from treaties.   See also art.34 of the 1969 Vienna Convention, "a treaty does not create either obligations or rights for a third state without its consent". As to when a treaty can produce obligations for a third state, see arts 35–38.

Amendments of a treaty

A treaty may be amended by agreements between the parties, art.39.

Article 40 sets out general principles applicable to the amendment of multilateral treaties and provides that any proposed amendments must be notified to all contracting states and each contracting state has the right to take part in:

(a) the decision as to the action to be taken in regard to such a proposal; and
(b) the negotiation and conclusion of any agreement for the amendment of the agreement.

Article 41 provides that two or more of the parties to a multilateral treaty may agree to modify the treaty as between themselves, alone, under certain conditions, e.g. provided for by the treaty or not prohibited by the treaty.

Validity of treaties

Under the 1969 Vienna Convention five grounds may be invoked to invalidate a treaty. This is an exhaustive list made of the following:

(a) Article 46 and 47: non-compliance with municipal law requirements;
(b) Article 48: error;
(c) Article 49 and 50: fraud and corruption;
(d) Article 51 and 52: coercion;
(e) Article 53: *jus cogens*.

Termination of; suspension of; and withdrawal from treaties

A treaty may be terminated, or the withdrawal of a party may take place, if done in accordance with the treaty or otherwise by consent, arts 54–59).

A material breach of a treaty is defined in art.60 as consisting of:

> "(a) a repudiation of the treaty not sanctioned by the present Convention; or
> (b) the violation of a provision essential to the accomplishment of the object or purpose of the treaty."

In the event of a **material** breach of a bilateral treaty, the non-guilty party may terminate it or suspend its operation in whole or in part, art.60(1). In respect of a multilateral treaty the non-guilty parties may, by unanimous agreement, suspend the operation of the treaty in whole or in part, or terminate it either: (i) between themselves and the defaulting state or (ii) as between all parties. Article 60(2)(b) and (c) make provision for action by a party specially affected by the breach and any other party, other than the defaulting state.

Note, art.60 paras 1–3 do not apply to provisions:

> "relating to the protection of the human person contained in treaties of a humanitarian character, in particular to provisions prohibiting any form of reprisals against persons protected by such treaties", art.60(5).

A treaty may also be terminated on grounds of supervening impossibility of performance, art.61, or fundamental change of circumstances, art.62.

In the *Fisheries Jurisdiction* case *(Jurisdiction)* (1974) I.C.J. Rep. 3 Iceland sought to terminate its 1961 Exchange of Notes with the UK. Under that Agreement either party could invoke the ICJ's jurisdiction to resolve a dispute arising from Iceland's extension of its fisheries zone. The UK had made such a reference to the ICJ and Iceland sought to rely on *rebus sic stantibus* to terminate the 1961 Agreement. However the ICJ highlighted that the change of circumstances:

> "must have been a fundamental one ... and [have] resulted in a radical transformation of the extent of the obligations still to be performed. The Change must have increased the burden of the obligations to be executed to the extent of rendering the performance something essentially different from that originally undertaken."

Also, in the case *Concerning the Gabcikovo-Nagymaros Project (Hungary/Slovakia)* (1997) (see above, p.14), it was stated that:

> "A fundamental change of circumstances must have been unforeseen; the existence of the circumstances at the time of the treaty's conclusion must have constituted an essential basis of the consent of the parties to be bound by the treaty. The negative and conditional wording of Article 62 ... is a clear indication moreover that the stability of treaty relations requires that the plea of fundamental change of circumstances be applied only in exceptional cases."

A treaty which is declared invalid is void. The provisions of a void treaty have no legal force, art.69.

RELATIONSHIP OF CUSTOMARY INTERNATIONAL LAW AND TREATY LAW

Customary international law and treaty law have equal authority in international law. If both exist regarding a disputed issue treaty law takes precedence.

In the *Wimbledon* case (1923) P.C.I.J. Rep., Series A, No. 1 it was held that Germany's sovereignty was not violated by art.380 of the Treaty of Versailles whereby the Kiel Canal was made an international waterway. This was because the restrictions on the exercise of Germany's sovereign rights were the result of entering into a treaty and accordingly the Treaty of Versailles provisions prevailed over Germany's neutrality regulations, which reflected customary international law.

Unless otherwise expressly intended the treaty provision will prevail over an earlier conflicting rule of customary international law for the parties concerned. However, a new rule of customary international law supersedes previous inconsistent treaty provision unless the contrary has been agreed.

In the *Nicaragua (Merits) case* (see above, p.9), the issue before the ICJ was whether customary international rules on armed force and intervention continued to apply, notwithstanding the existence of subsequent subsisting treaties, namely the UN Charter and other multilateral treaties to which the US and Nicaragua were parties. The need for the Court to seek an answer arose after the US entered a reservation excluding the Court's jurisdiction over, "disputes arising under a multi-lateral treaty." The Court stated:

> "There are no grounds for holding that when customary international law is comprised of rules identical to those of treaty law, the latter "supervenes" the former, so that the customary international law has no further existence of its own."

Amendment of customary international law by agreement happens regularly, whereas amendment of international agreements by custom is infrequent.

A treaty law will not be given precedence over *jus cogens*.

. . . .

ARTICLE 38 SOURCES OTHER THAN TREATY AND CUSTOM

General principles of law recognised by civilised nations

One of the best definitions of "general principles" is that of the late Professor Parry, *Sources and Evidences of International Law*, at 85:

> "(1) actual rules of international law which are, however, of so broad a description that it is not improper to call them principles, and
>
> (2) maxims ... of universal application in domestic law, which obviously ought to or must apply in the international sphere also".

In practice, general principles which have been applied are those found in major domestic legal systems and include:

The principle of *estoppel* (personal bar)—for example, in the *Temple of Preah Vihear case* (1962) I.C.J. Rep. 6, Thailand, having acquiesced in a map in which a temple was shown on the Cambodian side of the border was precluded from denying its earlier acceptance of the map.

No one must be a judge in his own cause—for example, see the *Mosul Boundary case* (1925) P.C.I.J. Rep., Series B, No. 12;

The principle of reparation—for example, in the *Chorzow Factory case (Jurisdiction)* (1927) P.C.I.J. Series A, No. 9, the PCIJ declared that, "it is a principle of international law that the breach of an engagement involves an obligation to make reparations." Subsequently, in the *Chorzow Factory case (Indemnity) (Merits)* (1928) P.C.I.J. Rep. Series A, No. 17, the PCIJ held that Poland was under an obligation to make reparations to the German Government.

The principle of a state's responsibility for all its agents—for example, see the *Fabiani case* (1896) 10 R.I.A.A. 83.

New areas of international law

Issues previously not dealt with by international law have demanded reference to domestic law. For example, see the *Barcelona Traction, Power and Light Company case*, (see above, p.9) at 37, where, in relation to an issue of company law, the ICJ held:

> "If the Court were to decide the case in disregard of the relevant institutions of municipal law it would, without justification, invite serious legal difficulties. It would lose touch with reality, for there are no corresponding institutions of international law to which the Court could resort. Thus the Court has, as indicated, not only to take cognisance of municipal law but also to refer to it."

Equity

In international law this is not a separate source of international law. However, in Judge Hudson's Separate Opinion in the *Diversion of Water from the Meuse case* (1937) P.C.I.J. Rep., Series A/B, No 70, 73–77, he stated that:

> "what are known as principles of equity have long been considered to constitute a part of international law, and as such they have often been applied by international tribunals".

He later stated that:

> "under Article 38 of the Statute, if not independently of that article, the Court has some freedom to consider principles of equity as part of the international law which it must apply."

Equity refers to the way in which the substantive law is applied and includes principles of fairness, reasonableness and justice.

Parties to a dispute may be directed to find a solution by reference to "equitable principles". Equitable principles have been used notably in Law of the Sea maritime delimitation cases, see e.g. *North Sea Continental Shelf cases* (see above, p.7) and *Tunisia v Libyan Arab Jamahiriya (Continental Shelf)* (1982) I.C.J. Rep. 18.

DEFINITION CHECKPOINT

Ex Aequo et Bono

Equity in this sense must be distinguished from deciding a case *ex aequo et bono* (according to what is right and good). Article 38(2) provides the ICJ with the power, if the parties to a contentious case agree, to take a decision on the basis of this provision over and above all other rules.

DEFINITION CHECKPOINT

Non Liquet

General principles were included to avoid *non liquet* situations. *Non liquet* is a doctrine whereby a judicial body could decline to decide a case on the grounds that no rules existed because of the international legal system's lack of development. The role of general principles has been to fill the gaps. As international law develops, such situations become less likely.

JUDICIAL DECISIONS

The International Court of Justice

DEFINITION CHECKPOINT

Stare Decisis

Also known as the doctrine of precedent, this means that previous judicial decisions bind courts in subsequent cases.

Generally, the doctrine of stare decisis does not apply in international law. Article 38(1)(d) is subject to art.59, which provides that a decision of the ICJ has no binding force except between the parties to the case and in respect of that particular case. However, previous decisions are examined and taken into account by the ICJ. The value of such practice is judicial consistency and certainty for the parties concerned.

Advisory Opinions

The ICJ is also competent to deliver Advisory Opinions on any legal question. Strictly speaking these are not binding but a number have made a notable influence on, and contribution to, the development of international law, e.g. *Reparations for Injuries Suffered in the Service of the United Nations* (1949) I.C.J. Rep. 185; *Advisory Opinion on Certain Expenses of the United Nations* (1962) I.C.J. Rep. 151; *Advisory Opinion on Western Sahara* (1975) I.C.J. Rep. 12; and *Legal Consequences of the Construction of a Wall in the Occupied Palestine Territory* (2004) 43 I.L.M. 1004. The *Advisory Opinion on Reparations* developed the concept of legal personality, while the case of the construction of the wall effectively identified obligations for Israel.

Decisions of other courts and tribunals

Article 38 does not limit "judicial decisions" only to those of the ICJ. Decisions of other international courts and tribunals may also be referred to, such as those of the International Criminal Tribunals for the former Yugoslavia and Rwanda, the ICC, hybrid tribunals such as the Special Court for Sierra Leone, and specialised courts such as the European Court of Human Rights. Also, decisions of national courts may provide evidence of how a particular issue is viewed by a state. Historically a number of national courts have been responsible for developing certain useful principles now recognised as international law, e.g. the United States Supreme Court on boundary issues.

. . . .

JUDICIAL WRITINGS

Writers played an important role in the early development of international law, e.g. Grotius, Vattel and Vitoria. The importance of the role of writers has now declined, but they still make a contribution by helping to establish state practice and highlighting, where appropriate, the need for international regulation. As to who is the most highly qualified remains open to debate. Writings and judicial decisions are on a "par" and one does not carry more weight than the other. Both are subsidiary sources which may be utilised.

OTHER POSSIBLE SOURCES OF INTERNATIONAL LAW

Article 38 is a product of its time and, given the rapid development of international law, there are other possible sources. Article 38 is therefore not exhaustive.

General Assembly Resolutions
General Assembly of the United Nations (192 Members).

The functions of the General Assembly (GA) are set out in arts 10, 11, 13 and 14 of the United Nations (UN) Charter. All Member States have one vote within the GA, art.18 of the UN Charter.

Only resolutions on budget and procedure are legally binding, art.18(2) and (3) of the UN Charter. Other resolutions are of no binding effect. Some resolutions, though, carry more moral weight than others, for example Declarations of Principle, i.e. Resolution 1514/49 (1960) Declaration on the Granting of Independence to Colonial Countries and Peoples (United Nations).

See also Judge Lauterpacht's Separate Opinion in *Voting Procedure on Questions Relating to Reports and Petitions Concerning the Territory of South West Africa* (1955) I.C.J. Rep. 67, where he stated:

> "It would be wholly inconsistent with sound principles of inter-
> pretation as well as with highest international interest, which can
> never be legally irrelevant, to reduce the value of the Resolutions
> of the General Assembly—one of the principal instrumentalities
> of the formation of the collective will and judgment of the com-
> munity of nations represented by the United Nations—and to
> treat them ... as nominal, insignificant and having no claim to
> influence the conduct of the Members. International interest
> demands that no judicial support, however indirect, be given to
> any such conception of the Resolution of the General Assembly
> as being of no consequence".

GA resolutions may also provide evidence as to the position adopted by a state on a particular issue, thus helping develop customary international law.

Security Council Resolutions
The Security Council is the principal organ of the UN with primary responsibility for the maintenance of international peace and security, art.24 of the
UN Charter. Every member of the 15 member Security Council possesses one
vote, art.27 of the UN Charter. Procedural matters are decided by a simple
majority, art.27(2) of the UN Charter. Non-procedural matters require the

affirmative vote of nine members, including the concurring vote of the five permanent Member States: China, France, Russia, the United Kingdom and the United States, art.27(3). Decisions of the Security Council are binding, art.25 of the UN Charter.

Regional Organisations

There now exist an increasing number of regional organisations dealing with a variety of subject matters, including human rights, trade and sustainable development. Such organisations include the Council of Europe (CoE), the European Union (EU), the Organisation of American States (OAS), the African Union (AU) and the League of Arab States (LAS).

The CoE was established in the wake of the Second World War "to promote common action in economic, social, cultural and related matters", art.1 of the Statute of the CoE. Ten original Member States signed the Statute of the Council on May 5, 1949. The current membership of the CoE stands at 47. The CoE is best known for its human rights activities and most notably the 1950 European Convention on Human Rights and Fundamental Freedoms. There now exists considerable jurisprudence on the European Convention which has emanated from the European Court of Human Rights.

The EU is a different type of regional organisation in that, in addition to its original economic objectives, it seeks to promote a closer union amongst Member States. The EU emerged from the European Economic Community (EEC), which had been established in 1957. The EU currently consists of 27 Member States and in the context of sources the European legal order is an independent legal order, which should be applied uniformly in all Member States.

Since December 1, 2009 when the Lisbon Treaty came into force, the EU acquired legal personality as a single entity. The Lisbon Treaty extends the use of the co-decision procedure—now called the "ordinary legislative procedure"—extending the powers of the European Parliament in the EU law-making process.

The OAS was provided for in the Pact of Bogotá in 1948. The OAS is considered a regional organisation for the purpose of the UN Charter and the OAS provides for peaceful settlement as well as promoting political and economic co-operation. The OAS has been influential in the promotion of human rights especially by way of the 1969 American Convention on Human Rights. The Inter-American Court of Human Rights has been responsible for the implementation and supervision of the 1969 American Convention on Human Rights and this has led to what is now a considerable volume of case law.

The AU is the successor to the Organisation of African Unity (OAU), which was established in 1963. The AU was established in 1999. Its objective is to promote regional co-operation.

Similarly, within the Arab Region, the LAS was set up in 1945 for the purpose of closer collaboration between members.

In addition to these regional organisations there are the Specialised Agencies of the UN, including the International Labour Organisation (ILO) and the World Health Organisation (WHO). The former has produced a substantial number of Conventions covering employment, whereas the latter seeks to promote the, "highest possible level of health" for all peoples. In the field of trade a leading body is the World Trade Organisation (WTO), established in 1995 with the responsibility of providing the common institutional framework for the conduct of trade relations.

Soft law

"Soft law" refers to non-legally binding international instruments. The term includes treaties which contain general obligations—"legal soft law"—as well as non-binding statements of intent, codes of conduct and statements, e.g. from professional bodies—"non-legal soft law".

Soft law must be in writing. Examples of soft law are the 1948 Universal Declaration of Human Rights and the 1992 Rio Declaration on the Environment and Development. The advantage of soft law is it can assist in promoting compromise and prevent deadlock. It may become "hard law", e.g. Universal Declaration provisions reflected in the 1966 UN International Covenants.

DEFINITION CHECKPOINT

Lex ferenda

"Non-legal soft law"; the law as it should be. Principles which are not currently law but which may become normative in the future. They become law through a subsequent treaty, rule of customary international law, or other law-making process. *Lex ferenda* can be compared with *lex lata*. This is hard law; the law as it exists.

International Law Commission (ILC)

Tasks—"progressive development of international law and its codification", art.13 of the UN Charter; Ch. II ILC Statute.

Progressive development is:

> "the preparation of draft conventions on subjects which have not yet been regulated by international law or in regard to which the law has not yet been sufficiently developed in the practice of States", art.15 of the ILC Statute.

Codification is:

> "the more precise formulation and systemisation of rules of international law in fields where there already has been extensive State practice, precedent and doctrine", art.15 of the ILC Statute.

The distinction between codification and progressive development is often blurred, see Ad Hoc Sorenson J. (Dissenting Opinion) in the *North Sea Continental Shelf case* (see above, p.7), stating:

> "It has come to be generally recognised, however, that this distinction between codification and progressive development may be difficult to apply rigorously to the facts of international legal relations. Although theoretically clear and distinguishable the two notions tend in practice to overlap or to leave between them an intermediate area in which it is not possible to indicate precisely where codification ends and progressive development begins. The very act of formulating or restating an existing customary rule may have the effect of defining its contents more precisely and removing such doubts as may have existed as to its exact scope or the modalities of its application."

Structure—the ILC is made up of 34 individuals who sit independently of their governments. The ILC meets for two, one–month sessions in the year. It usually initiates its own work programme although the General Assembly may request that it looks at a particular field of law.

Function—The ILC has been responsible for Conventions on a number of topics including treaties, e.g. 1969 Vienna Convention on the Law of Treaties; diplomatic relations, e.g. 1961 Vienna Convention on Diplomatic Relations; state responsibility, e.g. 2001 Draft articles on the Responsibility of States for Internationally Wrongful Acts 2001; and the ICC. Preparatory work of the ILC is important in identifying state practice.

Jus Cogens

Jus cogens refers to norms of international law which have peremptory force, which are binding and from which no derogation may be made except by another peremptory rule. The only definition of *jus cogens* is that provided in arts 53 and 64 of the Vienna Convention on the Law of Treaties 1969. A treaty provision contrary to a *jus cogens* norm is void, art.53 of the Vienna Convention. Whereas art.64 provides if a new *jus cogens* norm develops any existing treaty in conflict with that norm becomes void and terminates. A *jus cogens* norm is one accepted and recognised by the international community of states as a whole and may be found only in either a treaty or custom. Examples of *jus cogens* are the prohibition on the use of force, see *Nicaragua (Merits) case* (see above, p.9); the prohibition on genocide and torture; and denying self-determination.

See also *Siderman de Blake v Republic of Argentina* (1992) 965 F.2d 699, 717 (9th Cr.), where the Court said:

> "the right to be free from official torture is fundamental and universal, a right deserving of the highest status under international law, a norm of *jus cogens*".

Note, the Commentary of the International Law Commission 1966, ILC Articles on State Responsibility, Ch.3 of Part 2 "Serious Breaches of Obligations under Peremptory Norms of General International Law", arts 40 and 41. See also *The International Law Commission's Articles on State Responsibility— Introduction, Text and Commentaries*, Cambridge, 2002, Crawford, J., pp.242– 260.

Revision Checklist

You should now know and understand:

- The different sources of law used by the ICJ;

- The two elements required to form a rule of customary international law;

- Whether customary international law can develop from a treaty;

- Whether customary international law can develop from UN Resolutions;

- The advantages of treaty law over custom;

- The relationship between the sources listed in art.38(1) UN Charter;

- The main provisions of the 1969 Vienna Convention;

- The *pacta sunt servanda* principle;

- What is understood by a reservation;

- The circumstances under which reservations can be made;

- The grounds that may be invoked to invalidate a treaty;

- The significance of the ICJ's Advisory Opinion in the *Reservation to Genocide Convention case* to the law on reservations;

- The approach to treaty interpretation favoured by the 1969 Vienna Convention;

- The position of third states to treaties;

- The meaning of a fundamental change of circumstances;

- The importance of art.60(5) of the 1969 Vienna Convention;

- Other possible sources of international law not mentioned in art.38(1) UN Charter;

- What is understood by *jus cogens*.

QUESTION AND ANSWER

The Question

"Article 38(1) of the ICJ Statute does not mention sources yet it is regarded as an authoritative statement on the sources of international law."

Critically discuss

Advice and Answer

State what art.38(1) is, i.e. a direction to the ICJ and how it should deal with disputes raised before it. Article 38(1) has created a mechanism for the settlement of disputes. Identify the contents of art.38(1) and consider how and if it has become an authoritative statement. The relative value of each "source" should be detailed and discussed. Article 38(1) should also be placed in historical context and the question as to whether there are other possible sources of international law, outside art.38(1) should also be addressed. In conclusion state whether you agree/disagree with the proposition contained in the question.

Relationship Between Domestic and International Law

4

INTRODUCTION

What is the relationship between international law and domestic law? How a domestic legal system adopts international law is essentially a matter for the state. There is no prescribed uniform practice for states to follow and a state may adopt different stances towards international treaty law and customary international law.

The issue becomes of particular relevance when there is a perceived conflict and the state's domestic law is at odds with international law.

MONISM, DUALISM AND THE FITZMAURICE COMPROMISE

The two principal theories are the monistic and dualistic schools of thought.

Monism—Monists see international and domestic law as components of the same legal system and in the event of conflict, deference would be given to international law. A monistic country is one which accepts international law as part of its domestic law automatically.

Dualism—According to strict dualists international law and domestic law are two legal systems independent of each other. Their respective fields of operation are different and neither system has any impact on the other. Given this, dualists do not envisage a conflict between international and domestic law. A dualistic state is one which requires a specific act of incorporation for the international law to become part of domestic law.

The Fitzmaurice Compromise—This recognises that international and domestic law have separate areas of operation. However when there is an area of potential conflict, the conflict is one of legal obligation and not of legal systems.

In many states, e.g. the UK and the US, it is presumed the legislator does not intend to violate international law. See *PO v Estuary Radio* [1968] 2 Q.B. 740, C.A, for the UK.

DOMESTIC LAW FROM AN INTERNATIONAL PERSPECTIVE

International law is regarded as supreme. See art.13 of the Draft Declaration on Rights and Duties of States 1949, where:

> "each State has the duty to carry out in good faith its obligations arising from treaties and other sources of international law, and it may not invoke provisions in its constitution or its laws as an excuse for failure to perform this duty."

See also arts 27 and 46 of the Vienna Convention on the Law of Treaties 1969.

Article 27 states:

> "a party may not invoke the provisions of its internal law as justification for its failure to perform a treaty. This rule is without prejudice to Article 46".

Article 46 provides:

> (1) A State may not invoke the fact that its consent to be bound by a treaty has been expressed in violation of a provision of its internal law regarding competence to conclude treaties as invalidating its consent unless that violation was manifest and concerned a rule of its internal law of fundamental importance.
>
> (2) A violation is manifest if it would be objectively evident to any State conducting itself in the matter in accordance with normal practice and in good faith."

KEY CASE

ALABAMA ARBITRATION AWARDS MOORE, I INT. ARB. 495 (1872).
The case arose as a result of a claim by the US following damage caused by a number of vessels of which the Alabama was one. These vessels had been built and fitted in Great Britain for a private order, but in the knowledge that they were to be used by the Confederates during

the American Civil War. This, it was maintained, was contrary to Britain's neutrality in the Civil War. Britain alleged there was no rule within domestic legislation prohibiting such contracts. However the Arbitration Tribunal held that neither municipal legislative provisions nor the absence of municipal legislation could be pleaded successfully as a defence for non-fulfillment of international obligations. The Tribunal held " ... the Government of Her Britannic Majesty cannot justify itself for a failure in due diligence on the plea of insufficiency of the legal means of action which it possessed."

See also *Free Zones of Upper Savoy and Gex* (1932) P.C.I.J. Rep. Series A/B, No. 46.

INTERNATIONAL LAW FROM A DOMESTIC PERSPECTIVE

UK PRACTICE

The UK is monistic in respect of customary international law but dualistic in respect of treaty law.

Customary international law

Early attitude: see the *Buvot v Barbuit case* (1737) Cases, t. Talbot 281, in which Lord Talbot stated, "that the law of nations, in its full extent was part of the law of England." Endorsed by Lord Mansfield in *Triquet v Bath* (1746) 3 Burr 1478. See also *R v Keyn (The Franconia)* (1876) 2 Ex.D 63; *West Rand Central Gold Mining Co v R* [1905] 2 K.B. 391; and *Compania Naviera Vascongada v Cristina (The Cristina)* [1938] 1 All E.R. 719.

The UK position has been modified and is automatic incorporation unless there is a legislative measure or judicial decision of a higher court to the contrary, see *Chung Chi Cheung v R* [1939] A.C. 160; *Thakrar v Home Secretary* [1974] Q.B. 684; *Trendtex Trading Corporation v Central Bank of Nigeria* [1977] Q.B. 529, C.A.; and *R v Bow Street Metropolitan Stipendiary Magistrate Ex p. Pinochet Ugarte (No 1)* [2000] 1 A.C. 61, see also *Ex p. Pinochet (No 3) [2000] 1 A.C. 147*.

In the event of a conflict between customary international law and a British statute, the statute will be enforced, for example see the case of *Mortensen v Peters* (1906) 8 F. (J.) 93. In this case, Mortensen, the Danish Master of a Norwegian ship, was convicted by a Scottish Court for otter trawling in the Moray Firth, which was contrary to a by-law under the Herring Fishery (Scotland) Act 1889. The issue arose because part of the Moray Firth lies more than three miles from the coast of Scotland. Mortensen's offence took place in the area covered by the by-law but beyond the three-mile limit. Mortensen appealed against his conviction, his appeal was however unanimously dismissed. Lord Kyllachy stated:

> "—it may probably be conceded that there is always a certain presumption against the Legislature of a country asserting or assuming the existence of a territorial jurisdiction going clearly beyond limits established by the common consent of nations— that is to say, by international law ... But then it is only a presumption, and as such it must always give way to the language used if it is clear, and also to all counter presumptions which may legitimately be had in view in determining, on ordinary principles, the true meaning and intent of the legislation. Express words will of course be conclusive, and so also will plain implication."

Treaties

In the UK, treaty making is a competence of the executive within the Royal Prerogative. A treaty must be incorporated into British domestic law through an Enabling Act. An Enabling Act is a safeguard against potential abuse by the Executive.

For when an Enabling Act is required see *Parlement Belge* [1879] 4 P.D. 129, which stated:

> "If the Crown had power without the authority of parliament by this treaty to order ... This is a use of the treaty making prerogative of the Crown which I believe to be without precedent and in principle contrary to the laws of the constitution."

See also *Maclaine Watson v Department of Trade and Industry* [1988] 3 W.L.R. 1033, where:

> " ... the Royal prerogative whilst it embraces the making of treaties, does not extend to altering the law or conferring rights on individuals or depriving individuals of rights which they enjoy in domestic law without the intervention of parliament ... quite simply, a treaty is not part of English law unless and until it has been incorporated into the law by legislation."

Note, there is no need for an Enabling Act for conduct of hostilities and cession of territory.

> ### DEFINITION CHECKPOINT
>
> *The Ponsonby Rule*
> This is a constitutional Convention which requires the text of a signed treaty to be laid before Parliament for 21 days preceding ratification and publication in the UK Treaty Series.
>
> *Explanatory Memorandum*
> Since 1997, an Explanatory Memorandum has accompanied each treaty laid before Parliament in accordance with the Ponsonby Rule. An Explanatory memorandum identifies the principal elements of a treaty, assisting Members of Parliament to understand a treaty without referring to it directly.

The reception of treaty law in the UK was considered most frequently with respect to the European Convention on Human Rights (ECHR). This was prior to the **Human Rights Act 1998**, which was the Enabling Act giving effect to the ECHR within the UK.

However, Westminster legislative measures may be found to be incompatible with the Human Rights Act, see, e.g. House of Lords decision in *A & Others v Secretary of State for the Home Department; X & Another v Secretary of State for the Home Department* [2004] UKHL 56, where it was held s.23 of the **Anti-Terrorism, Crime and Security Act 2001**, was incompatible with arts 5 and 14 of ECHR. The courts cannot strike down incompatible legislation; they can only issue a Declaration of Incompatibility, see s.4 of the Human Rights Act 1998.

Executive certificate

This is a statement issued by the Foreign Office relating to, "certain categories of questions of fact in the field of international affairs". The Certificate is accepted by the courts as conclusive even in the face of contrary evidence. This is endorsed by s.21 of the **State Immunity Act 1978** and *Duff Development Co v Government of Kelantan* [1924] A.C. 797, in which the conclusive nature of executive certificates was based upon the rule of "best evidence" and to a lesser degree the doctrine whereby the Executive and the courts should adopt the same stance on matters of foreign affairs.

The conclusive nature of executive certificates is further endorsed in the case of *Carl Zeiss Stiftung v Rayner and Keeler (No 2)* [1967] A.C., which reaffirmed the position adopted in *Duff*.

However executive certificates are not conclusive regarding statutory interpretation or construction of documents, see *Re Al-Fin Corporation's Patent* [1971] Ch. 160, where as evidence of the judiciary's willingness to look beyond the executive certificate to determine the status of North Korea, it was stated there was, "no such rule of law restricting the evidence to be considered to that provided by the Foreign Office."

US PRACTICE

Custom

The US legal system is a member of the common law family and adopts an attitude similar to that of the UK, see cases such as *The Nercide* 9 Cr. 388 (US 1815); *The Paquete Habana* 175 US 677 (1900); *Filartiga v Pena-Irala* 630 F. 2d 786 (1980); and *United States v Fawaz Yunis* 30 I.L.M. 403 (1991).

In the *Paquete Habana* (see above) Mister Justice Grey stated:

> "International law is part of our law, and must be ascertained and administered by the courts of justice of appropriate jurisdiction, as often as questions of right depending upon it are duly presented for their determination."

However this acceptance of customary international law only applies provided there is no domestic judicial decision or legislative act to the contrary.

The case *of Filartiga v Pena-Irala (above)* held that:

> " ... for purposes of civil liability, the torturer has become like the pirate and slave trader before him *hostis humani generis*, an enemy of all mankind."

The position in the US today is as reflected in *United States v Fawaz Yunis (above)*, in which the court stated:

> "Statutes inconsistent with principles of customary international law may well lead to international law violations. But within the domestic legal realm, that inconsistent statute simply modifies or supersedes customary international law to the extent of the inconsistency."

Hence the US practice reflects that of the UK, i.e. the courts will apply domestic law even if allegedly contrary to customary international law.

Treaties

In the US the legislature is involved in the treaty making process. The President has, "Power by and with the advice and consent of the Senate, to make Treaties provided two-thirds of the Senators present concur," art.11(2) of the US Constitution.

The Senate participates in treaty making by exercising a check on the Executive. Treaty law is supreme in the US, see *Edye v Robertson* 112 US 580 (1884), in that it has the same status as an Act of Congress, but no more than an Act of Congress and is neither "irrepealable or unchangeable" and enjoys "no superiority over an Act of Congress." Acts of Congress are construed as conforming to international law. However, see *Diggs v Schultz* 470F (2d) 461 (1972), in which it was acknowledged that Congress could, if it wished, denounce treaties and could not be prevented from doing so by other branches of government. A treaty may be repealed or modified by an act of a later date.

Self-executing treaties and non-self executing treaties

A self-executing treaty is one which is automatically part of US domestic law in that no enabling act is required, whereas non self-executing treaties are only incorporated into domestic law pursuant to a specific act of incorporation, see *Foster and Elam v Neilson* 27 US (2 Pet.) 253 (1829).

Characteristics of self-executing treaties are—no uncertainty; no ambiguity; and not forward looking. In *Sei Fujii v California* 242 P. (2d) 617 (1952), it was stated that:

> "for a treaty provision to be operative without further imple-
> menting legislation and have statutory effect and force, it must
> appear that the framers of the treaty intended to prescribe a rule
> that, standing alone, would be enforceable in the courts."

Executive agreements

Executive agreements are international agreements entered into by the President without involving the Senate. They have the same force as a treaty and possess the same legal binding effect as treaties. For validity of such agreements see *US v Belmont* 301 US 324 (1937) and *US v Pink* 315 US 203 (1942).

Efforts to make executive agreements subject to greater congressional control are reflected in the Case Act 1972, as amended in 1977 and 1978.

State Department suggestions

Equivalent to the UK executive certificate but US courts treat them as persuasive and not conclusive.

TREATY MAKING WITHIN A FEDERAL STATE

A feature of the federal state is the division of competence between the central federal legislature and individual state legislatures. For problems that may arise see *Missouri v Holland* 252 US 416 (1920). This case highlights how a treaty making competence may become a form of indirect legislation bypassing constitutional constraints. In this case the US Supreme Court upheld the 1918 Act of Congress giving effect to a treaty, whereas federal legislation on the same subject matter was deemed ultra vires.

Compare this case with *AG for Canada v AG for Ontario* [1937] A.C. 326, which illustrates the problems which may be encountered when the treaty making competence lies with the federal government but the competence to give effect to the treaty obligation lies with individual state legislatures.

Revision Checklist

You should now know and understand:

- **The essence of monism and dualism;**
- **The consequences of characterising a state as dualistic;**
- **The Fitzmaurice Compromise;**
- **The UK approach to international law;**
- **The relevance of the decision in the *Alabama Claims Arbitration*;**
- **The Ponsonby Rule, and the reason for this practice;**
- **The significance of the Human Rights Act 1998;**
- **The US approach to international law;**
- **The differences between a self-executing treaty and a non-self executing treaty.**

QUESTION AND ANSWER

The Question

International law does not allow a state to invoke the legal procedures of its own municipal legal system as a justification for non-compliance with international rules.

Critically comment

Advice and Answer

The general subject matter of the question is the relationship of international law to domestic law. Initially theoretical background may be provided, i.e. the schools of thought may be identified—monism, dualism and harmonisation. The question then arises regarding primacy and the issue should be examined from an international law perspective. Relevant Conventions, arbitration and judicial decisions should be highlighted, e.g. the Vienna Convention on the Law of Treaties, *Alabama Claims Arbitration* and Free *Zones of Upper Savoy and Gex* case. The reason for the international law position should be highlighted. It may also be identified that acceptance or non-acceptance of international law is decided primarily by states and not prescribed by international law. The different approach adopted in respect of customary law and treaty law could be discussed and illustrated by reference to specific examples of municipal practice.

Territory

5

INTRODUCTION

Territory is the tangible evidence of state sovereignty. It is not possible to have a state without a territory, although the necessary territory may be very small. Within its territory a state has the right, "to exercise ... to the exclusion of any other State, the functions of a State", *Island of Palmas* case (1928) 2 R.I.A.A. 829, at 838.

The territory of a state includes the land mass, subsoil, the water enclosed therein, the land under that water, the seacoast to a certain limit and the airspace over the land mass and the territorial sea. There are a number of ways in which territory can be acquired. In contemporary international law, the way in which title is acquired is mostly of academic interest, unless title is disputed.

MEANS OF ACQUIRING TITLE TO TERRITORY

Occupation

Occupation refers to the method of obtaining original title to territory. It is the means by which territory that has not previously been appropriated may be acquired. Occupation is effective with regards to terra nullius.

DEFINITION CHECKPOINT
Terra nullius
Land belonging to no one; land which has never been subject to the sovereignty of a State.

The position of indigenous communities was clarified in the *Western Sahara* case, (see above, p.25) in which it was stated that the acquisition of sovereignty in respect of territories which were inhabited by tribes or peoples enjoying a social and political organisation, was not regarded as terra nullius, but rather was effected "through agreements concluded with local rulers." Such agreements with local rulers, whether or not considered as an actual "cession" of the territory, were regarded as derivative routes of title. In other words not original title obtained by terra nullius occupation.

Discovery in itself does not give good title to territory: discovery must be followed by "effective occupation".

Effective Occupation

This relates to the actual exercise of sovereignty. The display of sovereignty necessary will be determined by, e.g. geographical factors.

In the *Island of Palmas case* (above, p.41), the pronouncements made by Judge Huber—the sole arbitrator—on the nature of territorial sovereignty are still considered good law. The Philippines were ceded by Spain to the US at the end of the 1898 Spanish American War under the Treaty of Paris. However an American Official visited the Island of Palmas, thought by the US to be part of the ceded territory, and found the Dutch flag flying. The question of sovereignty over the Island of Palmas was subsequently submitted to arbitration. In respect to how territorial sovereignty may be displayed, Judge Huber stated at 840:

> "Manifestations of territorial sovereignty assume, it is true, different forms, according to conditions of time and place. Although continuous in principle, sovereignty cannot be exercised in fact at every moment on every point of a territory. The intermittence and discontinuity compatible with the maintenance of the right necessarily differ according as inhabited or uninhabited regions are involved, or regions enclosed within territories in which sovereignty is incontestably displayed or again regions accessible from, for instance the high seas."

In the *East Greenland case* (1933) P.C.I.J. Rep. Set A/B No. 53 22–147, at 46 it was noted by the Court that the exercise of minimal sovereign rights could be sufficient:

> "provided that the other state could not make out a superior claim. This is particularly true in the case of claims to sovereignty over areas in thinly populated or unsettled countries."

In the *Clipperton Island Arbitration* (1932) 26 A.J.I.L. the publication in English of the French claim reinforced an earlier declaration of sovereignty on behalf of France and was taken as sufficient to establish good title.

Effective occupation has to be established, open and public, involving continuous and peaceful display of state authority over a long period of time, see *Eritrea v Yemen* (1998) 114 I.L.R. 1 and *Island of Palmas* case (see above, p.41). See also the *Minquiers and Ecrehos case* (1953) I.C.J. Rep. 47. "Peaceful" refers to the display of sovereign authority without protest from other interested states. Evidence of state authority demonstrates intention (*animus*) to act as sovereign. In territorial claims focus has been placed on what is referred to as the "critical date". The importance of this is that the state showing an effective title immediately prior to that date has a superior claim. The critical date is determined by the responsible adjudicating body and will be determined by the particular circumstances of each case.

Prescription

Prescription is the means of establishing title to territory which is not terra nullius. Prescription legitimises an initially doubtful title provided there is a public display of state sovereignty and no other interested state objects. Protest from a claimant state or dispossessed sovereign can negate a prescriptive claim. See *Chamizal Arbitration (US v Mexico)* 5 A.J.I.L. (1911) 782; and *Kasikili/Sedulu Island (Botswana v Namibia)* (1999) I.C.J. Rep, 1045. The length of time necessary to provide a title by way of prescription is not set but rather depends on circumstances relevant in each case, e.g. geographical. No international tribunal has, as yet, found existence of title based exclusively on prescription.

Conquest

In contemporary international law territory cannot be acquired by the use of force or conquest. Conquest was the possession of enemy territory taken by military force. Effective conquest required the actual taking of territory and an intention to take over. See Draft Declaration on Rights and Duties of States 1949 and the 1970 General Assembly Declaration on Principles of International Law Concerning Friendly Relations and Co-Operation Among States in Accordance with the UN Charter. The doctrine of inter-temporal law demands that claims of sovereignty be viewed in the context of the rules of international law prevailing at the time at which the sovereignty claim is based. This was clearly spelt out in *Island of Palmas case* (see above, p.41), "[a] juridical fact must be appreciated in the light of the law contemporary with it, and not of the law in force at the time when a dispute in regard to it arises or falls to be settled."

Cession

This involves the peaceful transfer of territory from one sovereign to another. This is usually done via treaty and most frequently at the conclusion of hostilities, although could also be done by sale, e.g. Alaska to the US from Russia in 1867.

Note, the acquiring state cannot gain more rights over the land than rights possessed by the predecessor, *Island of Palmas case* (see above, p.41).

Accretion and Avulsion

These are geographical processes which seldom occur. Accretion describes a natural increase in territory, e.g. formation of alluvial deposits. Avulsion denotes a violent increase in territory through, e.g. volcanic action.

New States

When a state achieves independence in accordance with the principle of self-determination, it involves a transfer from one sovereign to another, thus giving derivative title to territory to the new sovereign.

> ### ▌DEFINITION CHECKPOINT
>
> *Uti possidetis*
> The boundaries of former colonies are deemed to constitute the boundaries of newly independent successor states. In *Frontier Dispute (Burkina Faso v. Mali)* (1986) I.C.J. Rep, 554, the Court confirmed that, "[*uti possidetis*] is a general principle, which is logically connected with the phenomenon of obtaining independence, wherever it occurs. Its obvious purpose is to prevent the independence and stability of new states being endangered by fratricidal struggles provoked by the changing of frontiers following the withdrawal of the administering power".

POLAR REGIONS

Arctic

The Arctic is mainly ice and as such is incapable of occupation in the traditional sense. Certain states exercise sovereign rights in respect of Arctic areas, e.g. Denmark over Greenland. Certain environmental protection measures have been adopted by Arctic states (Canada, Denmark, Finland, Iceland, Norway, Sweden, the US and Russia) seeking to guarantee the sustainable and equitable development of the Arctic area, e.g. Arctic Environmental Protection Strategy 1991 now subsumed by the Arctic Council since 1997, ALTA Declaration 1997 and Arctic Environmental Impact Assessment (ARIA) which was adopted under ALTA.

Antarctica

All of Antarctica has been the subject of territorial claims. Article 1 of the Antarctica Convention 1959 provides that Antarctica is to be used exclusively for peaceful purposes and any military activity is prohibited. There are a number of initiatives, which have been adopted regarding environmental protection, e.g. the 1991 Madrid Protocol on Environmental Protection to the Antarctic Treaty.

AIRSPACE

States possess exclusive sovereignty over airspace. This includes the airspace above territory and territorial waters. See the 1919 Paris Convention on the Regulation of Ariel Navigation and the 1944 Chicago Convention on International Civil Aviation. Article 1 of the Chicago Convention states that, "the Contracting States recognise that every State has complete and exclusive sovereignty over the airspace above its territory." This Convention applies to civil aircraft, art.3, and not to state aircraft, which includes aircraft used in military, customs and police services. Article 6 provides that permission must be sought before flying into or over the territory of a contracting state. It is also recognised that permission may carry conditions. The Chicago Convention is supplemented by the International Air Services Transit Agreement (Two Freedoms Agreement) which relates to flyover rights and landing for non-traffic purposes, e.g. refuelling. The International Air Transport Agreement (Five Freedoms Agreement) which includes the Two Freedoms plus traffic rights such as:

> "(3) The privilege to put down passengers, mail or cargo taken on in the territory of the State whose nationality the aircraft possesses; (4) The privilege to take on passengers mail and cargo destined for the territory of the State whose nationality the aircraft possesses; (5) The privilege to take on passengers mail and cargo destined for the territory of any other contracting State and the privilege to put down passengers, mail and cargo coming from any such territory."

However the Five Freedoms Agreement has not been widely ratified and most air traffic is regulated by a network of bilateral and multilateral agreements.

OUTER SPACE

The UN Committee on the Peaceful uses of Outer Space was established in 1958 and is the body charged with the regulation of outer space activity. Two principles govern such activities, namely that outer space be used only for peaceful means and that it is the common heritage of mankind. For example see the 1967 Treaty on Principles Governing the Activities of States in the

Exploration and Use of Outer Space including the Moon and Other Celestial Bodies (Outer Space Treaty), which provides at art.1 that:

> "the exploration and use of outer space, including the moon and other celestial bodies, shall be carried out for the benefit and in the interests of all countries, irrespective of their degree of economic or scientific development, and shall be the province of all mankind."

Article 2 provides that:

> "outer space, including the moon and other celestial bodies, is not subject to national appropriation by claim of sovereignty, by means of use or occupation, or by any other means."

Of particular note is the prohibition contained in art.4 regarding the establishment of military bases and the installation of nuclear weapons or any other kinds of weapons of mass destruction. Under art.9, states are charged with the responsibility of avoiding, "harmful contamination and also adverse changes in the environment of the Earth resulting from the introduction of extra terrestrial matter."

The Outer Space Treaty has been revised and elaborated upon by the 1979 Agreement Concerning the Activities of States on the Moon and Other Celestial Bodies (Moon Agreement). This treaty reinforces that the moon is not subject to national appropriation by any claim of sovereignty, by means of use or occupation, or by any other means. Article 11(7)(d) of the Moon Agreement highlights the need to achieve:

> "an equitable sharing by all States Parties in the benefits derived from those resources, whereby the interests and needs of the developing countries, as well as the efforts of those countries which have contributed either directly or indirectly to the exploration of the moon, shall be given special consideration."

The 1968 Agreement on the Rescue of Astronauts, the Return of Astronauts and the Return of Objects Launched into Outer Space; the Convention on International Liability for Damage Caused by Space Objects 1972; and the Convention on the Registration of Objects Launched into Outer Space 1975 have further supplemented the measures pertaining to outer space.

The 1972 Convention was referred to in the *Cosmos 954 Claim* (1979) 18 I.L.M. 899, brought by Canada against the USSR. The claim arose when a nuclear powered Soviet satellite broke up in Canadian airspace. Canada claimed compensation of six million Canadian dollars for the clean up of the affected area however the matter was eventually settled on payment of three million Canadian dollars. The latter was paid without the admission of liability.

Revision Checklist

You should now know and understand:

- The different ways in which title to territory may be acquired;

- The issues of discovery and good title to territory;

- The importance of *animus*;

- The different ways in which sovereignty can be displayed;

- The importance of the Arbiter's decision in the *Island of Palmas case*;

- The difference between prescription and occupation;

- The unique position of the Arctic;

- The nature of a state's sovereignty over its airspace;

- The significance of the 2 Freedoms Agreement and the 5 Freedoms Agreement;

- The principle governing the regulation of outer space.

QUESTION AND ANSWER

The Question

How may title to territory be acquired in international law?

Advice and Answer

A straightforward question to which the answer should identify the various means whereby title to territory may be acquired. The importance of acquiring title to territory may also be identified. Reference should be made to the relevant case law when appropriate, e.g. the *Clipperton Island* case, and the *Island of Palmas* case. The question as to whether all the traditionally accepted modes of acquiring territory are still valid may be addressed.

TERRITORY

International Personality: Part 1 (States)

INTRODUCTION

Entities in possession of international personality are accordingly subjects of international law. As such they owe responsibilities to the international community and enjoy rights, the benefits of which may be claimed and which, if denied, may be enforced to the extent recognised by the international legal system.

> **DEFINITION CHECKPOINT**
> *International Personality*
> The possession of international rights and duties and the procedural capacity to seek redress for alleged violations. Entities with international personality can also be held accountable for non-fulfilment of duties.

> **KEY CASE**
>
> REPARATION FOR INJURIES SUFFERED IN THE SERVICE OF THE UNITED NATIONS, (above p.25):
>
> "The subjects of law in any legal system are not necessarily identical in their nature or in the extent of their rights, and their nature depends upon the needs of the community. Throughout its history, the development of international law ... and the progressive increase in the collective activities of States has already given rise to instances of action upon the international plane by certain entities which are not States."

States are the primary and original subjects of international law and all states possess full international legal personality. That is, every state possesses the totality of rights and duties under international law and international personality is an inherent attribute of statehood. The personality of states is original whereas that of other entities is derivative.

The predominance of states is borne out by the following factors:

- Only states may be parties to a contentious case before the International Court of Justice, art.34 ICJ Statute;
- the nationality of claims rule; and
- the state is deemed to have suffered the alleged wrong.

See *Mavrommatis Palestine Concession case* [1924] P.C.I.J. Rep. Series A, No. 2 12, in which the ICJ stated:

> "It is true that the dispute was at first between a private person and a State—i.e. between M. Mavroamtis and Great Britain. Subsequently, the Greek Government took up the case. The dispute then entered upon a new phase; it entered the domain of international law, and became a dispute between two States ... by taking up the case of one of its subjects and by resorting to diplomatic action or international judicial proceedings on his behalf, a State is in reality asserting its own rights—its right to ensure, in the persons of its subject, respect for the roles of international law ... once a State has taken up a case on behalf of one of its subjects before an international tribunal, in the eyes of the latter the State is sole claimant."

A state does not generally act as agent of an individual, see *Civilian War Claimants Association Limited v the King* [1932] A.C. 14 H.L., endorsing that international law does not require a state to hand over compensation to a claimant.

. . . .

REQUIREMENTS OF STATEHOOD

The requirements of statehood set out in art.1 of the Montevideo Convention on the Rights and Duties of States 1933 are:

- a permanent population;
- a defined territory;
- government; and
- the ability to enter into relations with other states

This is regarded as reflecting customary international law. See also *Opinion Number 1*, the Arbitration Commission of the European Conference on Yugoslavia, 1991, where, "the State is commonly defined as a community which consists of a territory and a population subject to an organized political authority" and, "such a State is characterised by sovereignty".

However no minimum population is required nor is there a prescribed geographical size and boundaries need not be definitively established. See *North Sea Continental Shelf* cases (see above p.7):

> "There is for instance no rule that the land frontiers of a State must be fully delimited and defined, and often in various places and for long periods they are not ... "

There is a need for an effective government. "Effective" means independent and enjoying legislative and administrative competence. See International Committee of Jurists 1920, Report on the Status of Finland, where it was stated:

> "until a stable political organisation had been created, and until the public authorities had become strong enough to assert themselves throughout the territories of the State without the assistance of foreign troops."

Note, the absence of an effective regime does not negate statehood, e.g. Somalia.

Capacity to enter into relations with other states

This is different from the other (factual) criteria in that it depends upon the response of the states within the international community. An entity may have the capacity to enter into relations but may be denied the opportunity if other states decline to have relations with it.

Self-determination

The principle whereby the political future of a colony or similar non-independent territory is determined in accordance with the wishes of its inhabitants. See, e.g. Resolution 15/1514 (1960) Declaration on the Granting of Independence to Colonial Territories and Peoples (United Nations), stating self-determination to be a right, whereby all peoples can, "freely determine their political status and freely pursue their economic, social and cultural development." See also *Western Sahara case* (see above, p.25), in which the Court defined the principle of self-determination, " ... as the need to pay regard to the freely expressed will of peoples ... ".

Resolution 15/1514 (*above*) was forward looking in providing that independence was to be attained in accordance with self-determination. Note also the International Covenants on Civil and Political Rights, and on

Economic, Social and Cultural Rights 1966, Common art.1, which provides, "all peoples have the right of self-determination. By virtue of that right they freely determine their political status and freely pursue their economic, social and cultural development."

Note, self-determination is regarded as a legal right within the colonial context. However that is the extent of the right and it is:

> "well established that, whatever the circumstances, the right to self-determination must not involve changes to existing frontiers at the time of independence (*uti possidetis juris, see above p.44*) except where the States agree otherwise",

Opinion Number 2, the Arbitration Commission of the European Conference on Yugoslavia 1992. This reflects para 6 Resolution 15/1514 (see above, p.50), which reinforces the principle of national unity and territorial integrity and states:

> "[a]ny attempt aimed at the partial or total disruption of the national unity and the territorial integrity of a country is incompatible with the purposes and principles of the Charter of the United Nations."

KEY CASE

RE REFERENCE BY THE GOVERNOR IN COUNCIL CONCERNING CERTAIN QUESTIONS RELATING TO THE SECESSION OF QUEBEC FROM CANADA (1998) 161 D.L.R. (4TH) 385.

The question before the Court was whether Quebec possessed a right under Canadian Constitutional Law or international law to secede unilaterally from Canada. The Court denied the existence of such a right and held that self-determination could only arise in limited circumstances and that there is not a right existing under international law whereby entities within an existing State may secede unilaterally.

For discussion of the relationship between self-determination and *uti possidetis juris* see *Frontier Dispute (Burkino/Faso Mali)* (1986) I.C.J., Rep. 554.

See also the Declaration on the Guidelines on the Recognition of New States in Eastern Europe and the Soviet Union (1992), which emphasises human rights and the rights of minorities. The following criteria were set out:

- "Respect for the provisions of the Charter of the United Nations and the commitments subscribed to in the Final Act of Helsinki and in the Charter of Paris, especially with regard to the rule of law, democracy and human rights;
- Guarantees for the rights of ethnic and national groups and minorities in accordance with the commitments subscribed to in the framework CSCE;
- Respect for the inviolability of all frontiers which can only be changed by peaceful means and by common agreement;
- Acceptance of all relevant commitments with regard to disarmament and nuclear non-proliferation as well as to security and regional stability;
- Commitment to settle by agreement, including where appropriate by recourse to arbitration, all questions concerning State succession and regional disputes.

The Community and its Member States will not recognise entities, which are the result of aggression. They would take account of the effects of recognition on neighbouring States."

RECOGNITION OF STATES/GOVERNMENTS

Recognition as a state is the formal acknowledgement by an existing state that the recognised entity possesses the relevant criteria of statehood.

Recognition of a government is the formal acknowledgement by an existing state that the recognised regime is the effective government.

There are two leading schools of thought, namely, the constitutive and the declaratory/evidentiary.

Constitutive theory—Supporters of this school maintain that the international personality of the entity in question is established through the act of recognition.

Declaratory/evidentiary theory—According to this school of thought recognition is seen as no more than the formal acknowledgement of an existing set of circumstances. This is regarded as more in keeping with state practice. See *Opinion Number 1* (see above, p.49), where it provides, " ... the existence or disappearance of the State is a question of fact; that the effects of recognition by other States are purely declaratory."

Note, recognition is also retroactive, see *Luther v Sagor* [1921] 3 K.B. 532, C.A., see below.

As a rule an entity will be recognised as a state once. It is not the norm for recognition, once afforded, to be withdrawn if that is the criteria of statehood the state continues to subsist. If they do not, and the state no longer exists, de-recognition is not required.

In contrast, recognition of a governmental regime is independent from recognition of a state. Recognition may be withheld from a regime without affecting the existence of the relevant state. The issue of recognition is important when the regime has assumed power by unconstitutional means, e.g. a coup d'état.

Note, 1977 US Statement, which said:

> " ... in recent years, US practice has been to de-emphasise and avoid the use of recognition in cases of changes of government and to concern ourselves with the question of whether we wish to have diplomatic relations with the new governments.
> The Administration's policy is that establishment of relations does not involve approval or disapproval but merely demonstrates a willingness on our part to conduct our affairs with other governments directly."

Also note the 1980 UK Government announcement which stated:

> " ... we have conducted a re-examination of British policy and practice concerning the recognition of Governments. This has included a comparison with the practice of our partners and allies. On the basis of this review we have decided that we shall no longer accord recognition to Governments."

The reason for this policy being that "recognition" was interpreted as denoting approval, e.g. of a regime which has assumed power by unconstitutional means.

Judicial guidance on whether a government should be recognised was given in *Somalia (A Republic) v Woodhouse Drake & Carey (Suisse) SA* [1993] 1 All E.R. 371. Factors to be taken into account include: whether the government in question is the constitutional government; the stability and scope of administrative control; what dealings, if any, the British government has with the regime; and, in marginal cases, the response of other members of the international community. See also *Sierra Leone Telecommunications v*

Barclays Bank Plc [1998] 2 All E.R. 821, in which the previous case was followed and the criteria laid down, therein, applied.

DE JURE / DE FACTO RECOGNITION

In effect such recognition denotes how the entity is recognised rather than a description of the recognition. The essence of the distinction was that an entity recognised as de facto—existing as a matter of fact—possessed most of the necessary components of sovereignty, whereas a de jure (existing as a matter of law) entity possessed complete sovereignty. The distinction applied more regularly to governments than to states and emerged through British practice in the nineteenth century. However, the distinction is now of minimal importance given the decrease in explicit recognition.

De facto is not an alternative to de jure but rather a safeguard against premature recognition.

Recognition is essentially a political act, a discretionary act of the Executive, which produces legal consequences.

EFFECTS OF RECOGNITION

The legal effect of recognition is that an entity is recognised as a state.

Recognition of an entity as a state affords it the full totality of rights and duties inherent in statehood. These include sovereignty (e.g. territorial, jurisdictional); the duties to respect the rights of other states to refrain from the use of force—save in defined circumstances; and the responsibility for acts carried out on its behalf. There is no period of grace for new states. Therefore when an entity becomes a state it immediately assumes all the attributes of statehood and cannot plead its youthfulness for non-fulfillment of its international obligations.

KEY CASE

LUTHER V SAGOR (ABOVE, SEE P.53)
The issue was regarding recognition of a 1919 Soviet Government decree nationalising a factory in the USSR. The defendant company bought wood from the new Soviet Government in 1920. The Russian company, which had owned the factory prior to 1919, claimed title to the wood on the grounds that the 1919 Nationalisation Decree should

not be recognised by an English Court because the UK Government had not recognised the Soviet Government. In the Court of First Instance judgement was given in favour of the plaintiff, however, appeal was made by the defendants to the Court of Appeal. The UK Government recognised the Soviet Government in 1921 and recognition was back-dated to December 1917 when the Soviet authorities assumed control from the Provisional Government. It was concluded in the Court of Appeal that the Court "must treat the Soviet Government, which the Government of this country has now recognised as the *de facto* Government of Russia, as having commenced its existence at a date anterior to any date material to the dispute between the parties to this appeal."

Legal consequences of recognition within the UK are:

(i) A recognised state or government has locus standi (the right of a party to appear and be heard before a court) in British courts and can raise a legal action.

(ii) A recognised state is entitled to immunity in the UK: See *The Arantzu Mendi* case [1939] A.C. 256, HL, in which the nationalist Government of Spain under General Franco was recognised as "a Government which at present exercises de facto administrative control over the larger portion of Spain."

(iii) A recognised state's legislative and administrative acts are given effect within the UK: See *Luther v Sagor* (see above, p.53).

(iv) Recognition of the state is retroactive to the date of the entity's establishment: See *Luther v Sagor* (see above, p.53) and *Gdynia Ameryka Linie Zeglugowespolka Akcyjina v Boguslawski* [1953] A.C. 11. The latter case highlights how retroactivity can create a problem within the context of de jure/de facto recognition and that a de facto and de jure entity can exist simultaneously. The House of Lords in that case stated it was:

> "not inconsistent to say that the recognition of the new government has certain retroactive effects, but that the recognition of the old government remains effective down to the date when it was in fact withdrawn."

What is important is that recognition is given retroactive effect so as to give validity to acts of the previously unrecognised regime rather than invalidating the acts of the previously recognised de jure regime.

Points (i) to (iv) are shared by de jure and de facto entities.

De jure recognition alone implies full diplomatic relations and the right to recover a public debt or state asset, endorsed by *Fenton Textiles Association v Krassin* (1922) 38 T.L.R. 259; and *Haile Selassie v Cable and Wireless Ltd (No 2)* [1939] Ch. 182.

EFFECTS OF NON-RECOGNITION

Internationally, an unrecognised entity is not allowed to act as it chooses. See, e.g. the Pueblo Incident 1968. The danger of giving *carte blanche* to unrecognised entities should be all too obvious.

In respect of the UK there is no locus standi, no immunity from jurisdiction of British courts, and legislative and administrative measures cannot be denied effect. See *Somalia (A Republic) v Woodhouse Drake & Carey (Suisse) SA* (see above, p.53). Non-recognition can also have adverse effects for private persons or foreign companies. See *Adams v Adams* [1971] P. 188 in which a divorce decree of a Rhodesian Court, appointed by the Smith Regime, was not recognised under English law. This was resolved by the passing of an Order in Council, which gave effect to such personal status decrees. See also Lord Denning *obiter dicta* in *Hesperides Hotels v Aegean Holidays Ltd* [1978] Q.B. 205, CA, for supporting mitigating application of non-recognition in instances which had consequences for private individuals in their day to day affairs, such as marriages, divorces, leases and occupations.

In the case of *Carl Zeiss Stiftung v Rayner and Keeler* (see above, p.36) 855 the House of Lords resolved the issue by employing a legal fiction and held that the Soviet Union was the de jure authority in respect of East Germany and the unrecognised regime of East Germany was the subordinate body of the Soviet Government. Similarly in *Gur Corporation v Trust Bank of Africa Ltd* [1987] Q.B. 599 when the Ciskei Government, unrecognised by the UK, was treated as a subordinate body of the South African Government.

HOW RECOGNITION MAY BE ACCORDED

Implied

There is no list of prescribed acts implying recognition. What is important is intention. Initiation of diplomatic relations between a state and the relevant entity implies recognition, as does entering into a bi-lateral treaty on a general matter, e.g. a commercial topic. Participation in an international conference does not imply recognition, nor is the UN a recognising body for the international community. Membership of the UN is an acknowledgement that the entity fulfils the criteria for purposes of the UN only.

Express

As previously stated, now seldom used.

STATE SUCCESSION

Complex issues can arise when a new state appears and takes over from an existing state. What is the position for instance regarding previously existing treaties and is the new authority liable for the debts of the old authority?

State succession can be briefly defined as the replacement of one state by another in the responsibility of the international relations of territory.

DEFINITION CHECKPOINT

Guidance on State Succession

There is no formal role or procedure for state succession at the UN. In response to the problems presented by the break-up of British India, the UN Legal Affairs Committee developed three principles to serve as guiding principles for future cases:

> "1. That, as a general rule, it is in conformity with legal principles to presume that a State which is a Member of the Organization of the United Nations does not cease to be a Member simply because its Constitution or its frontier have been subjected to changes, and that the extinction of the State as a legal personality recognized in the International order must be shown before its rights and obligations can be considered thereby to have ceased to exist.
> 2. That when a new State is created, whatever may be the territory and the populations which it comprises and whether or not they formed part of a State Member of the United Nations, it cannot under the system of the Charter claim the status of a Member of the United Nations *unless it has been formally admitted* as such in conformity with the provisions of the Charter.
> 3. Beyond that, each case must be judged according to its merits."

U.N. GAOR, 1st Comm., Annex 14g, at 582-83, U.N. Doc. A/C.1/212 (1947) (letter from Chairman of the Sixth Committee to the Chairman of the First Committee).

Following the break-up of the Soviet Union, the Russian Federation presented itself as the continuation of the USSR's membership in the UN, and continued to occupy the permanent seat on the Security Council. The UN's acceptance of the Russian position was based on Russia possessing the majority of the land and population of the former state.

The Federal Republic of Yugoslavia (FRY), constituted of Serbia and Montenegro, unsuccessfully sought to succeed to the Socialist Federal Republic of Yugoslavia's (SFRY) seat at the UN. The Security Council recommended against FRY's claim, highlighting that FRY did not constitute either a majority of SFRY's land or population. There was no devolution agreement between SFRY and FRY regarding succession and there was general objection in the UN to the succession. As a result, FRY was required to formally request membership to the UN. FRY applied for membership and was admitted to the UN in 2000, later changing its name, in 2003, to Serbia and Montenegro.

In May 2006 Montenegro held a referendum and declared itself independent of Serbia. The following month Montenegro was accepted as a Member State of the UN by General Assembly Resolution 60/264.

The other four states of SFRY, Croatia, Bosnia-Herzegovina, Macedonia, and Slovenia applied for membership of the UN independently. All were accepted as members in 1992, with the exception of Macedonia, which gained membership in 1993 under the provisional name of the Former Yugoslav Republic of Macedonia, following Greek objections to the use of what it considers to be a Hellenic name.

Another area which may give rise to concern is succession to treaty obligations. As a norm the "clean slate principle" is favoured. In other words a successor state is not bound by the obligations undertaken by its predecessor. A successor state can, of course, assume the obligations of its predecessor should it wish to do so.

In respect of bilateral treaties, continuation by the successor state depends upon agreement between the successor state and the other party to the treaty.

Note however the "clean slate principle" does not apply in respect of treaties delimiting boundaries and creating territorial regimes, or to those which impose restrictions on a treaty for the benefit of another state.

The rules relating to treaties have been spelt out in the 1978 Vienna Convention on the Succession of States in Respect of Treaties. This Convention is seen as representing progressive development as it takes account, primarily, of the newer states.

Human rights treaties have been the subject of discussion particularly in the context of the break-up of Former Yugoslavia. The Human Rights committee in 1992 stated that, "all the peoples within the territory of the former Yugoslavia are entitled to the guarantees of the Covenant." The

Covenant refers to the International Covenant on Civil and Political Rights (ICCPR). In 1997 in General Comment Number 26, the Human Rights Committee stated quite clearly that:

> "once the people are accorded the protection of the rights under the Covenant, such protection devolves with territory and continues to belong to them, notwithstanding change in government ... or State succession."

See also the separate opinions of Judge Shahabuddeen and that of Judge Weeramantry in the *Application of the Genocide Convention (Bosnia Herzegovina v Yugoslavia)* case (1996) I.C.J. Rep. 595. The former Judge expressed the view:

> "to effectuate its object and purpose, the [Genocide] Convention would fall to be construed as implying the expression of a unilateral undertaking by each party to the Convention to treat successor States as continuing as from independence any status which the predecessor State has as a party to the Convention."

Judge Weeramantry supported the existence of:

> "a principle of contemporary international law that there is automatic State succession to so vital a human rights Convention as the Genocide Convention."

Regarding debts these are dealt with along with state property and archives in the 1983 Vienna Convention on Succession of States in Respect of Property, Archives and Debt.

Revision Checklist

You should now know and understand:

- What is understood by legal personality;
- What is understood by international legal personality;
- Where the definition of international legal personality was articulated;
- Which entities possess original personality;
- What is understood by derivative personality;
- Which entities possess derivative personality;

- What constitutes a state;

- The two main schools of thought on recognition;

- The distinguishing features between the two schools of thought;

- The consequences of recognition within the UK's domestic legal system.

QUESTION AND ANSWER

The Question

What criteria require to be satisfied before an entity will be characterised as a state?

Advice and Answer

The answer would begin with the Montevideo Convention 1933 and the indices of statehood articulated therein. The answer should also consider the possibility of other criteria such as fulfilment of international human rights obligations. The consequences of recognition could be considered, as could the debate whether an entity has the legal right to be recognised as a state.

International Personality: Part 2 (International Organisations, etc.)

7

INTRODUCTION

States remain the primary subjects of international law, however they are no longer the only subjects. Other entities also have a degree of international personality. Of these the most important are international organisations, which dramatically increased in number during the twenty-first century. Individuals and other non-state actors may also possess a degree of international personality.

The international personality of states is an inherent attribute of their statehood, and is thus often referred to as *original*. Other subjects of international law possess international personality to the extent permitted by states, and is thus referred to as *derivative*.

INTERNATIONAL ORGANISATIONS

An international organisation, in international law, is one established by agreement and has states as its members. The most widely known organisation is the UN.

Figure 1: Main Organs of the UN

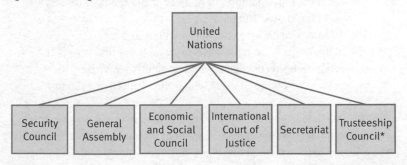

* Suspended in 1994

Today there are also many regional organisations, e.g. the Council of Europe and the Organisation of American States.

Competences of organisations vary and accordingly the international personality of these organisations varies. The key to determining this personality is the organisation's constituent document. This document may expressly establish legal personality, e.g. art.47 of the Treaty of European Union (ex-article 281 EC Treaty), or alternatively, and more usually, legal personality will be implied in the constituent document and consolidated through the practice of the organisation, e.g. the UN.

Article 104 of the Charter of the UN establishes the legal capacity of the organisation in the national law of Member States. However it does not mention the international legal personality of the UN. Article 105 deals with the privileges and immunities of the organisation and its agents, and is supplemented by the Convention on the Privileges and Immunities of the United Nations 1946, to which the UN and every Member State is a party. The Convention is concerned with the functional privileges and immunities from jurisdiction of the UN and its agents within Member States. See also Headquarters Agreements—e.g. The Headquarters Agreement Between the UN and the USA 1947.

KEY CASE

REPARATIONS FOR INJURIES SUFFERED IN THE SERVICE OF THE UNITED NATIONS (ADVISORY OPINION) (1949) I.C.J. REP. 174.

The ICJ was asked by the General Assembly to give an advisory opinion on whether the UN, following injury to one of its agents sustained in the performance of his duties, has:

"(i) ... the capacity to bring an international claim against the responsible de jure or de facto government with a view to obtaining the reparation in respect of the damage caused
(a) to the United Nations,
(b) to the victim or to persons entitled to him?
(ii) In the event of an affirmative reply on point i(b), how is the action to be reconciled with such rights as may be possessed by the State of which the victim is a national?"

The ICJ unanimously gave an affirmative response to i(a). In giving this response the ICJ made a general statement on the subjects of law and how in any legal system subjects are not necessarily identical in their nature or in the extent of their rights:

" ... their nature depends upon the needs of the community. Throughout its history, the development of international law ... and the progressive increase in the collective activities of States has already given rise to instances of action upon the international plane by certain entities which are not States."

In reaching its opinion the ICJ highlighted that the objectives of the UN could not be fulfilled in the absence of international personality and characterised the personality as "objective" in that the UN possesses personality which may be enforced vis-à-vis all members of the international community:

"In the opinion of the Court the Organisation was intended to exercise and enjoy, and is in fact exercising and enjoying, functions and rights which can only be explained on the basis of possession of a large measure of international personality and the capacity to operate upon an international plane. It is at present the supreme type of international Organisation and it could not carry out the intentions of its founders if it was devoid of international personality. It must be acknowledged that its Members, by entrusting certain functions to it, with the attendant duties and responsibilities, have clothed it with the competence required to enable those functions to be effectively discharged."

However although finding the UN to be an international person the ICJ emphasised:

"That is not the same thing as saying it is a State, which it certainly is not, or that its legal personality and rights and duties are the same as those of a State. Still less is it the same thing as saying that it is "a super-State", whatever that expression may mean. It does not even imply that all its rights and duties must be upon the international plane, any more than all the rights and duties of a State must be upon that plane. What it does mean is that it is a subject of international law and capable of possessing international rights and duties, and that it has the capacity to maintain its rights by bringing international claims."

In differentiating an organisation from a state the ICJ noted that:

"Whereas a State possesses the totality of international rights and duties recognised by international law, the rights and duties of an entity such as the Organisation must depend upon its purposes and functions as specified or implied in its constituent documents and developed in practice. The functions of the Organisation are of such a character that they could not be effectively discharged if they involved the concurrent action, on the international plane, of fifty-eight or more Foreign Offices ... the members have endowed the Organisation to bring international claims when necessitated by the discharge of its functions ...”

In respect of question i(b) the ICJ concluded that the UN possessed the legal capacity to afford protection to its agents. The ICJ expressed the view that such protection had to be afforded so as to assure the agent and:

“To ensure the independence of the agent, and, consequently, the independent action of the Organisation itself, it is essential that in performing his duties he need not have to rely on any other protection than that of the Organisation.”

The ICJ then had to deal with the question as to whether the UN had the capacity to bring a claim in reparation against a state that was not a member of the UN. The ICJ held in the affirmative stating:

“that fifty States, representing the vast majority of the members of the international community had the power, in conformity with international law, to bring into being an entity possessing objective international personality and not merely personality recognised by them alone, together with capacity to bring international claims.”

Having dealt with question (i) in the affirmative the ICJ then addressed the issue of possible priority between the diplomatic protection rights of the victim’s national State and the functional protection rights of the UN and the ICJ observed, “there was no necessary order of priority.”

DEFINITION CHECKPOINT

The Principle of Speciality
International organisations vary in the international personality possessed and in this respect their personality is distinct from the personality enjoyed by states.
  In the *Legality of the Use by a State of Nuclear Weapons in Armed*

Conflict (Advisory Opinion) (1996) 35 I.L.M. 809, the ICJ emphasised that:

> " ... international organisations do not, unlike States, possess a general competence, but are governed by the "principle of speciality", that is to say, they are invested by the States which create them with powers, the limits of which are a function of the common interest whose promotion those States entrust to them."

The organisation in question was the World Health Organisation (WHO) and in respect to that body the ICJ concluded that the:

> "responsibilities of the WHO are necessarily restricted to the sphere of public "health' ... and questions concerning the use of force ... are within the competence of the United Nations and lie outside that of special agencies."

INDIVIDUALS

Increasingly, the international rights and duties of individuals are being recognised.

Rights of individuals

Human rights have increasingly been extended to individuals since 1948. Prior to that the protection afforded to individuals was on an ad hoc basis, e.g. Minority Treaties concluded after the First World War providing protection for Albanians, Finns and Poles. See also the 1923 International Convention for the Suppression of Traffic of Women and Children; and the 1926 Slavery Convention. Only in the aftermath of the Second World War was there a concerted effort to provide protection on a comprehensive basis. Now there are many international human rights instruments providing protection against specific reprehensible types of behaviour, e.g. racial discrimination, and/or extending protection to groups perceived as vulnerable, e.g. children.

Duties of individuals

Historically there were very few international duties placed on individuals. However, customary international law has long recognised the duty on individuals not to be pirates. This duty still exists see arts 14–25 of the

Geneva Convention on the High Seas 1958 and arts 15–22 of the Law of the Sea Convention 1982.

Increasingly, individuals can no longer hide behind the apparatus of the state. At the 1946 Nuremberg Tribunal it was stated that:

> "crimes against international law are committed by men, not by abstract entities, and only by punishing individuals who commit such crime can the provisions of international law be enforced."

Article IV of the 1948 Convention on the Prevention and Punishment of the Crime of Genocide provides that:

> "persons committing genocide or any of the other acts enumerated in art.III shall be punished whether they are constitutionally responsible rulers, public officials or private individuals."

See also the Statute of the International Tribunal for the Prosecution of Persons Responsible for Serious Violations of International Humanitarian Law Committed in the Territory of the Former Yugoslavia, 1993 (ICTY), arts 1–7 of which set out the jurisdiction of the Court and provide that the Tribunal has jurisdiction over natural persons and individual criminal responsibility. Similarly, see arts 1–6 of the Statute of the International Tribunal for the Prosecution of Persons Responsible for Genocide and Other Serious Violations of International Humanitarian Law Committed in the Territory of Rwanda and Rwandan Citizens Responsible for Genocide and Other Such Violations Committed in the Territory of Neighbouring States, between 1 January 1994 and 31 December 1994 (ICTR).

In the Rome Statute 1998, which established an International Criminal Court, art.25(1) states that, "the Court shall have jurisdiction over natural persons pursuant to this Statute" and art.25(2) continues that:

> "A person who commits a crime within the jurisdiction of the Court shall be individually responsible and liable for punishment in accordance with this Statute."

Note, art.27(1) further provides, "This Statute shall apply equally to all persons without any distinction based on official capacity."

Individuals may also be held responsible for "grave breaches" of the 1949 Geneva Red Cross Conventions; 1977 Additional Protocols I and II; and also for the commission of such acts such as drug trafficking, terrorism and acts against state diplomats.

Procedural capacity of individuals

Individuals have limited procedural capacity and enjoy only that capacity given to them by states. States have been traditionally reticent in granting such procedural capacity. That said, in the *Danzig Railway Officials* case (1928) P.C.I.J. Rep., Ser. B, No. 15 4–47, it was acknowledged that:

> "the very object of an international agreement, according to the intention of the contracting parties, may be the adoption by the parties of some definite rules creating individual rights and obligations and enforceable by the national courts."

The tribunal established by the Upper Silesian Convention 1922 is notable as it allowed individuals to bring cases against their state of nationality, see *Steiner and Gross v Polish State* (1928) 4 A.D. 291.

In contemporary international law individuals enjoy much wider procedural capacity. For example, individuals have procedural capacity under the Optional Protocol to the International Covenant on Civil and Political Rights (ICCPR), which entered into force in 1976, in respect of alleged violations of rights set out in the Covenant. Article 1 of the Optional Protocol provides:

> "A State Party to the Covenant that becomes a party to the present Protocol recognises the competence of the Committee to receive and consider communications from individuals subject to its jurisdiction who claim to be victims of a violation by that State Party of the rights set forth in the Covenant. No communication shall be received by the Committee if it concerns a State Party to the Covenant which is not a party to the present Protocol."

Article 14(1) of the 1966 International Convention on the Elimination of All Forms of Racial Discrimination (ICEFRD) provides:

> "A State Party may at any time declare that it recognises the competence of the Committee to receive and consider communications from individuals or groups of individuals within its jurisdiction claiming to be victims of a violation by that State Party of any of the rights set forth in this Convention. No communication shall be received by the Committee if it concerns a State Party which has not made such a declaration."

Similar provisions can be found at art.22 of the Convention Against Torture 1984, and art.31 of the International Convention for the Protection of all Persons from Enforced Disappearance 2006.

The Optional Protocols to the International Covenant on Economic, Social and Cultural Rights 1966 (ICESCR), adopted in 2008; the Convention on the Elimination of Discrimination Against Women 1979 (CEDAW), adopted in 1999; and the Convention on the Rights of People with Disabilities 2006 (CRPD), adopted in 2006, also provide for individual petitions.

At a regional level, the European Convention on Human Rights, arts 34 and 35, and the American Convention on Human Rights, art.44, accept complaints from individuals. Individuals also have limited procedural capacity before the Court of Justice of the European Union, see art.263 of the Treaty on the Functioning of the European Union, which extends the previous art.230 EC Treaty.

OTHER NON-STATE ACTORS

There are other actors on the international arena, which are not subjects of international law, yet enjoy a degree of international personality. They enjoy such personality because states allow them to do so.

Rebel Groups
Rebel groups are relevant to international law in a number of ways. For example, they may have de facto control over territory and accordingly enter into international agreements and possibly arbitration, see e.g. *the Abyei Arbitration* Final Decision of the Permanent Court of Arbitration (2009). Also, in the conduct of armed conflicts, rebel groups are bound by international humanitarian law, see Common art.3 of the four Geneva Conventions 1949 and Additional Protocol II 1977. Further, "an insurrectional or other movement" will be held internationally responsible for its actions if it becomes the new Government of a state, see art.10 of the Draft articles on State Responsibility 2001.

The Holy See and the Sovereign Order of Malta
The Holy See is an anomaly in that it has a population, which is not permanent or indigenous, and its exclusive purpose for existence is religious. Notwithstanding this, it is party to a number of international treaties and enjoys permanent observer status within the UN as well as being present in organisations such as the ILO and WHO.

The Sovereign Order of Malta is a charitable organisation with headquarters in Rome.

Non-Governmental Organisations (NGOs)

Unlike international organisations, NGOs are established by individuals under domestic law. NGOs proliferated in number at the end of the twentieth century, and address a full spectrum of issues. Although some NGOs have a global reach and impact, they are not subjects of international law. However, over 3000 such organisations have consultative status before the UN Economic and Social Council, in accordance with art.71 UN Charter. Increasingly NGOs have been involved in treaty-making conferences, e.g. NGOs attended the sessions of the Preparatory Committee that produced a draft statute on the establishment of the International Criminal Court.

Of particular note is the International Committee of the Red Cross, which has a hybrid nature. Although it was constituted under Swiss law, it has been given a number of specific competencies under the 1949 Geneva Conventions.

Multinational Corporations

Many multinational corporations wield extensive power on the international arena, sometimes even more than states. Given this power, there have been calls for multinational corporations to exercise corporate accountability, and that this should take place within the international legal system. Indeed, many multinational corporations have voluntarily established corporate codes of conduct. However, the value of such codes is questionable given that the authors are simultaneously their addressees. An issue of growing importance is that of human rights violations due to adverse corporate activities, see e.g. the discussions surrounding the *Wiwa et al v Royal Dutch Petroleum et al* law suits (settled out of court, June 8, 2009) and the *UNOCAL case* (*Doe v Unocal Corporation et al*, Decision September 18, 2002).

Revision Checklist

You should now know and understand:

- The role of an international organisation's constituent document in determining international legal personality;

- The reasons why it was decided that the UN must have international personality;

- The principle of speciality; the significance of the *Reparation for Injuries* Advisory Opinion; and the significance of the *Nuclear Weapons* Advisory Opinion;

- Some of the international duties incumbent on individuals;

- The relative importance of the ICTY and the ICTR to the ICC;

- The extent to which individuals can seek redress within the international legal system;

- The dynamic nature of the concept of international personality;

- The role and position of some non-state actors within the international legal order.

QUESTION AND ANSWER

The Question

International personality is neither a static nor uniform concept.

Evaluate

Advice and Answer

Initially the term international personality should be defined. Reference should be made to the *Reparation* case. The answer demands charting the evolution of the concept from embracing only states to include other entities. The fact states remain the primary international actors should be acknowledged and supported by evidence, e.g. only states can be party to contentious cases before the ICJ. The emergence of international organisations and the rights/duties now incumbent on individuals should be illustrated and reference made to the procedural capacity of individuals. Distinction will be drawn between original and derivative personality. The answer should conclude by showing that the nature of the international legal system is such that new international "persons" have to be accommodated.

Law of the Sea

8

INTRODUCTION

The law of the sea is made up of those rules, which regulate relations between, primarily, states in respect of maritime matters. These rules have evolved from custom and treaty.

TREATY HIGHLIGHTER

The 1958 Geneva Conventions on the Law of the Sea (1958 Convention) were the product of work undertaken by the International Law Commission (ILC) and finally concluded at the First UN Conference on the Law of the Sea (UNCLOS I):

- Convention on the Territorial Sea and Contiguous Zone
- Convention on the High Seas
- Convention on the Continental Shelf
- Convention on Fishing and Conservation of Living Resources of the High Seas

These four Conventions codified existing customary international law, although certain provisions represented progressive development, e.g. continental shelf provisions.

The second UNCLOS was held in 1960 where the main issue was the breadth of the territorial sea and fishery limits. However no Convention was produced on that occasion.

TREATY HIGHLIGHTER

UNCLOS III
UNCLOS III had its opening session in 1973 but it was not until 1982 that the UN Convention on the Law of the Sea (1982 Convention) was produced. The 1982 Convention is an extensive document and includes all issues dealt with in 1958 as well as introducing some new features. There is also a provision relating to dispute settlement. The 1982 Convention entered into force November 16, 1994.

Note that all references to articles below are to those in the 1982 Convention.

. . . .

DEFINITION CHECKPOINT

Territorial Sea

> "Every State has the right to establish the breadth of its territorial sea up to a limit not exceeding 12 nautical miles, measured from baselines determined in accordance with this Convention", (art.3).

Previously the "territorial sea" had not been defined as state practice varied, with the norm being within 3–12 miles. The 12–mile limit has now been accepted as customary international law, see *Guinea/Guinea-Bissau Maritime Delimitation* case (1988) 77 I.L.R. 636.

Article 4 prescribes the outer limit of the territorial sea as the line:

> "every point of which is at a distance from the nearest point of the baseline equal to the breadth of the territorial sea."

The normal baseline, for measuring the breadth of the territorial sea is, except where otherwise provided by the convention, "the low water line along the coast as marked on large scale charts officially recognised by the coastal State", art.5.

Derogation is, however, allowed to take account of geography, for instance art.7(1) provides:

> "[i]n localities where the coastline is deeply indented and cut into, or if there is a fringe of islands along the coast in its immediate vicinity, the method of straight baselines joining appropriate points may be employed in drawing the baseline from which the breadth of the territorial sea is measured."

KEY CASE

ANGLO–NORWEGIAN FISHERIES CASE (1951) I.C.J. REP. 116
In this case the Court endorsed the legitimacy of the straight baseline system and indeed the Court's judgement was reflected in the 1958 and 1982 Conventions. However, the Court emphasised:

> "there is one consideration not to be overlooked, the scope of which extends beyond purely geographical factors: that of certain economic interests peculiar to a region, the reality and importance of which are clearly evidenced by a long usage."

See also art.7(5) of the 1982 Convention.

Article 10 sets out particular rules applicable to bays which belong to a single state, and defines a bay for the purpose of the 1982 Convention. The article provides a mechanism whereby straight baselines may be employed. However the provisions of art.10 do not apply to "historic" bays, art.10(6).

For the delimitation of territorial seas between opposite or adjacent states, see art.15. In which one of three methods may be employed; by agreement; by the median line; or by some other line necessary by reason of historic title or other special circumstances.

Both the 1958 and 1982 Conventions provide a definition of an island, however the 1982 Convention goes further and provides a legal regime of islands, art.121. See also the Court of Arbitration case *Concerning Delimitation of Maritime Areas (St Pierre and Miquelon)* (1992) 31 I.L.M. 1145, and the *Jan Meyen case (Denmark v Norway)* I.C.J. Rep. 1993 38, in which it was said that art.121 reflected, "the present status of international law." The importance of art.121 is that it restricts the circumstances in which an island may have an exclusive economic zone or continental shelf.

ARCHIPELAGIC STATES

For the purposes of the Convention an archipelago state is one made up, "wholly by one or more archipelagos and may include other islands." In art.46 Archipelago refers to:

> "a group of islands, including parts of islands, inter-connecting waters and other natural features which are so closely inter-related that such islands, waters and other natural features form an intrinsic geographical, economic and political entity, or which historically have been regarded as such."

Archipelagic states are dealt with specifically in the 1982 Convention in arts 46–54. These articles relate to base lines, legal status and the right of archipelagic sea-lane passages.

CONTIGUOUS ZONE

A contiguous zone is optional for a coastal state but if claimed must not exceed 24 nautical miles from the base lines from which the breadth of the territorial sea is measured, art.33(2). In a contiguous zone the coastal state may exercise the control necessary to:

"(a) prevent infringement of its customs, fiscal, immigration or sanitary laws and regulations within its territory or territorial seas and (b) punish infringement of the above laws and regulations committed within its territory or territorial seas."

INNOCENT PASSAGE

Coastal states are required to allow innocent passage through the territorial sea for specific purposes, by ships of all states whether coastal or land-locked, art.17(1). Innocent passage is defined in art.18 as:

"navigation through the territorial sea for the purpose of (a) traversing that sea without entering internal waters or calling at a roadstead or port facility outside internal waters or (b) proceeding to or from internal waters or a call at such roadstead or port facility."

Passage is to be continuous and expeditious, although stopping and anchoring is allowed but only in so far as it is incidental to ordinary navigation necessary by force majeure or distress or for the purpose of rendering assistance, art.18(2).

Passage is regarded as innocent provided it is not prejudicial to the peace, good order or security of the coastal state. Passage is not innocent if any of the activities set out in art.19(2)(a)–(l) are undertaken. Namely:

"(a) any threat or use of force against the sovereignty, territorial integrity or political independence of the coastal State, or in any other manner in violation of the principles of international law embodied in the charter of the United Nations;
(b) any exercise or practice with weapons of any kind;
(c) any act aimed at collecting information to the prejudice of the defence or security of the coastal state;
(d) any act of propaganda aimed at affecting the defence or security of the coastal state;
(e) the launching, landing or taking on board of any aircraft;

(f) the launching, landing or taking on board of any military device;

(g) the loading or unloading of any commodity, currency or person contrary to the customs, fiscal, immigration or sanitary laws and regulations of the coastal state;

(h) any act of wilful and serious pollution contrary to this Convention;

(i) any fishing activities;

(j) the carrying out of research or survey activities;

(k) any act aimed at interfering with any system of communication or any other facilities or installations of the coastal state; and

(l) any other activity not having a direct bearing on passage."

See also the *Corfu Channel case (Merits)* (1949) I.C.J. Rep.4, where it was said, "States in time of peace have a right to send their warships through straits used for international navigation between two parts of the high seas without the previous authorisation of a coastal state, provided that the passage is innocent."

A coastal state may take the steps necessary to prevent passage, which is not innocent, art.25. Foreign vessels are under an obligation to comply with the coastal state's laws and regulations. This is dealt with extensively in art.21 of the 1982 Convention.

Vessels engaged in innocent passage are only subject to the coastal state's criminal and civil jurisdiction in defined situations, in art.27:

"(a) if the consequences of the crime extend to the coastal state; or

(b) if the crime is of a kind to disturb the peace of the country, the good order of the territorial sea; or

(c) if the assistance of the local authorities has been requested by the captain of the ship, the consul of the country whose flag the ship flies; or

(d) if it is necessary for the suppression of illicit traffic in narcotic drugs (or psychotropic substances—1982 Convention only)."

The foregoing do not affect the right of the coastal state to take any steps authorised by its laws for the purpose of an arrest or investigation onboard a foreign ship passing through the territorial sea after leaving internal waters, art.27 (2).

Civil jurisdiction may only be exercised within the terms of art.28.

Note, the jurisdictional immunity enjoyed by warships and government vessels operated for non-commercial purposes is unaffected by arts 27 and 28. Rules applicable to warships and government vessels operated for non-commercial purposes are set out in arts 29–32.

Straits which are used for international navigation are the subject of arts 34–45.

EXCLUSIVE ECONOMIC ZONE (EEZ) ARTS 55–75

The 1982 Convention recognises the, "specific legal regime of the exclusive economic zone". The EEZ refers to that area beyond and adjacent to the territorial sea not extending beyond 200 nautical miles from the base lines from which the breadth of the territorial sea is measured, arts 55 and 57.

The coastal state has, within the EEZ, the sovereign rights of exploration, exploitation, conservation and management of natural resources, whether living or non-living, of the water superjacent to the seabed and of the seabed and its subsoil. It also has sovereign rights with regard to other activities for the economic exploitation and exploration of the zone, such as the production of energy from the water, currents and winds, art.56(1)(a).

The coastal state enjoys jurisdiction with regard to:

- the establishment and use of artificial islands, installations and structures;
- marine scientific research; and
- the protection and preservation of the marine environment, art.56(1)(b).

Article 58 spells out the rights and duties of other states in the EEZ, e.g. navigation and over-flight. It provides that in the exercise of these rights and performance of these duties, states are to have due regard to the rights and duties of the coastal state, and shall comply with the laws and regulations adopted by the coastal state in accordance with the 1982 Convention and other rules of international law compatible with the 1982 Convention. The coastal state is responsible for determining the allowable catch of living resources in its EEZ, art.61, and is responsible for promoting optimum utilisation of such living resources, art.62(1). The coastal state is also responsible for determining its capacity to harvest the living resources of the EEZ and, where it does not have the capacity to harvest the entire allowable catch, to make access arrangements for other states, art.62(2).

The rights of landlocked and geographically disadvantaged states are recognised by arts 69 and 70.

■ DEFINITION CHECKPOINT

The Continental Shelf

This is defined as comprising the sea bed and subsoil of the submarine areas that extend beyond a state's territorial sea throughout the natural prolongation of its land territory to the outer edge of the continental margin, or to a distance of 200 nautical miles from the baselines from which the breadth of the territorial sea is measured where the outer edge of the continental margin does not extend up to that distance, art.76(1). The continental shelf of a coastal state shall not extend beyond the limits prescribed in art.76(4)–(6).

Coastal States rights over the continental shelf

These are sovereign rights of exploration and exploitation of natural resources, art.77(1).

A coastal state's rights are exclusive in that no activity may be undertaken within the continental shelf without the express consent of the coastal state, art.77(2). The coastal state also enjoys the exclusive right to authorise and regulate drilling on the continental shelf for all purposes, art.81.

Note the coastal state's continental shelf rights do not affect the legal status of the superjacent waters or of the airspace above those waters. The exercise of coastal state rights over the continental shelf must not infringe or result in any unjustifiable interference with navigation and other rights and freedoms of other states provided in art.78.

Delimitation between states with opposite or adjacent coasts

Article 83 provides that such delimitation is to "be effected by agreement ... in order to achieve an equitable solution". See *Continental Shelf (Libyan Arab Jamahiriya v Malta) case* (see above, p.9), in which it was agreed by the parties that the delimitation of the continental shelf had to be effected by the application of equitable principles in all the relevant circumstances.

See also the *Continental Shelf case (Tunisia v Libya)* (1981) I.C.J. Rep. 3; *Gulf of Maine case* (1984) I.C.J. Rep. 246; *North Sea Continental Shelf case* (see above, p.7); *English Channel Arbitration* (1979) 18 I.L.M. 397; and *Guinea/Guinea-Bissau Maritime Delimitation case* (see above, p.72).

DEEP SEABED

The importance of the deep seabed is that it is rich in resources, e.g. manganese nodules. Furthermore technological advances are such that the issue of access to the deep seabed has had to be addressed.

The 1982 Convention sets out a regime representing a compromise for developing and developed states, namely:

- Resources are the common heritage of mankind;
- Activities in the area are to be undertaken for the benefit of mankind as a whole;
- No state is to claim or exercise sovereignty, or sovereign rights over the area;
- The area is to be used exclusively for peaceful purposes;
- Exploration and exploitation are to be done under the auspices of the International Seabed Authority (for further information see arts 156–188, however with respect to Pt XI of the 1982 Convention see General Assembly Resolution and Agreement 48/263 adopted in 1994 Relating to the Implementation of Pt XI of the UN Convention on the Law of the Sea—modifying Pt XI in relation to the deep sea);
- The International Tribunal for the Law of the Sea, provided for in art.288, has jurisdiction over any dispute concerning the interpretation and application of the 1982 Convention. See also the Seabed Disputes Chamber of the Tribunal. Relatively few states have accepted the jurisdiction of the Tribunal, and this is reflected in the low caseload.

HIGH SEAS

> **DEFINITION CHECKPOINT**
>
> *High Seas*
> Article 86 defines these as, "all parts of the sea that are not included in the exclusive economic zone, in the territorial sea, or in the internal waters of a State, or in the archipelagic waters of an archipelagic State."

Article 87 maintains the basic principle of freedom of the high seas, namely, the high seas are open to all states whether coastal or landlocked. The freedom of the high seas comprises freedom inter alia:

- of navigation;

- of over-flight;
- to lay submarine cables and pipelines;
- to construct artificial islands and other installations permitted under international law;
- of fishing; and
- of scientific research.

The foregoing list is not exhaustive and all freedoms are to be exercised with due regard to the interests of other states pursuant to their exercise of the freedom of the high seas, art.87(2).

Article 88 provides that the high seas are to be reserved for peaceful purposes and no state may validly purport to subject any part of the high seas to its sovereignty, art.89.

Articles 90–92 deal with the nationality of ships and their flags. Under art.90, "Every State, whether coastal or landlocked, has the right to sail ships flying its flag on the high seas". Article 91 leaves it to every state to set the conditions for the grant of its nationality to ships; the registration of ships in its territory; and the circumstances for flying its flag. Ships possess the nationality of the state whose flag they are entitled to fly. Although discretion is left to the state art.91 demands that a genuine link must exist between the state and the ship. Article 91(2) provides that the right to fly a state's flag shall be endorsed by documentation to that effect. A ship may only sail under the flag of one state and normally is subject to that state's exclusive jurisdiction. Article 92(2) aims to "defeat" the practice of flags of convenience.

Article 94 sets out the duties of the flag state and provides that every state "shall effectively exercise its jurisdiction and control in administrative, technical and social matters over ships flying its flag."

Warships on the high seas have complete immunity from jurisdiction of any state other than the flag state, as do ships owned or operated by a state used only on government non-commercial service.

Article 99 prohibits the transport of slaves.

Article 100 imposes a duty on all states to co-operate in the repression of piracy on the high seas or in any other place outside the jurisdiction of any state. Piracy is defined in art.101 as:

> "(a) any illegal acts of violence or detention, or any act of depredation, committed for private ends by the crew or the passengers of a private ship or a private aircraft, and directed: (i) on the high seas, against another ship or aircraft, or against persons or property on board such ship or aircraft; (ii) against a ship, aircraft, or property in a place outside the jurisdiction of any State;

(b) any act of voluntary participation in the operation of a ship or of an aircraft with knowledge of facts making it a pirate ship or aircraft;

(c) any act of inciting or of intentionally facilitating an act described in sub-paragraph (a) or (b)."

Article 108 calls upon states to co-operate in the suppression of illicit traffic in narcotic drugs and psychotropic substances engaged in by ships on the high seas, contrary to international Conventions. Article 109 requires states to co-operate in the suppression of unauthorised broadcasting from the high seas.

Article 110 deals with a warship's right of visit and provides that boarding a foreign ship, other than a ship entitled to complete immunity, is not justified:

"Unless there is reasonable ground for suspecting that,

(a) the ship is engaged in piracy;

(b) the ship is engaged in the slave trade;

(c) the ship is engaged in unauthorised broadcasting and the flag state of the warship has jurisdiction under Article 109;

(d) the ship is without nationality; or

(e) though flying a foreign flag or refusing to show its flag, the ship is in reality, of the same nationality as the warship."

HOT PURSUIT

Article 111 sets out when the right of hot pursuit may be employed. Hot pursuit may be undertaken when the competent authorities of the coastal state have good reason to believe the ship has violated the laws and regulations of that state. It must begin when the foreign ship or one of its boats is within the internal waters, the archipelagic waters, the territorial sea or the contiguous zone of the pursuing state. It may only be continued outside the territorial sea or the contiguous zone if the pursuit has not been interrupted. If the foreign ship is within a contiguous zone the pursuit may only be undertaken if there has been a violation of the rights for the protection of which the zone was established. The right of hot pursuit ceases as soon as the ship pursued enters the territorial sea of its own state or that of a third state. It may only be commenced after a visual or auditory signal has been given and may only be exercised by warships, military aircraft and or those clearly marked and identified as being on government service.

All states are entitled to lay submarine cables and pipelines on the bed of the high seas beyond the continental shelf, art.112(1). This entitlement however is subject to art.79(5) which calls upon states to have due regard to cables or pipelines already in position.

The right to fish on the high seas is subject to treaty obligations and to the rights and duties as well as to the interests of coastal states as provided in the 1982 Convention.

Article 118 requires states to co-operate in the conservation and management of living resources in the areas of the high seas.

For provisions on protection and preservation of the marine environment, see arts 192–238. States have the obligation to protect and preserve the marine environment, art.192, and the sovereign right to exploit their natural resources pursuant to their environmental policies and in accordance with their duty to protect and preserve the marine environment, art.193.

Figure 2: Zones Recognised by the International Law of the Sea

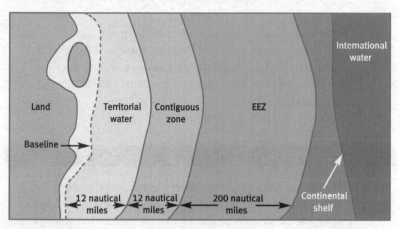

Note the above diagram represents an aerial view

Revision Checklist

You should now know and understand:

- The four Conventions which make up the 1958 Geneva Conventions;
- Which Convention currently regulates the law of the sea;
- The issues addressed for the first time by the 1982 Convention;
- The limit of the territorial sea;
- The limit of the contiguous zone;
- What is understood by the right of innocent passage;

- The nature of a coastal state's rights in the EEZ;
- The nature of a coastal state's rights in the continental shelf;
- What is understood by hot pursuit;
- The freedoms of the high seas.

QUESTION AND ANSWER

The Question

You are a member of the legal team of the newly independent Arys and your advice is sought on the following:

a) How Arys should claim and define its territorial sea;
b) The legal consequences of making such a claim and in particular whether neighbouring Beberry's fishing fleet can be excluded from entering Arys's territorial sea for any purpose; and
c) Should Arys claim a contiguous zone.

Advice and the Answer

a) In writing the memorandum reference should be made to the relevant provisions of the 1958 Geneva Conventions, the 1982 UN Convention on the Law of the Sea and customary international law. The geographical area to which the term territorial sea applies should be explained as should the general rules employed to measure the territorial sea. It is important to consider the possibility of Arys having an indented coastline. Consideration may also be given to the delimitation of the territorial sea between opposite or adjacent states and also the position of archipelagic states.
b) The nature of a coastal state's rights over the territorial sea and the obligations of the coastal state in relation to innocent passage require to be considered. The legal nature of the rights enjoyed by the coastal state should also be considered.
c) The relevant provisions of the 1958 Geneva Convention and the 1982 Convention should be invoked to explain the contiguous zone, what it is and the nature of the rights enjoyed therein.

State Responsibility

9

INTRODUCTION

State responsibility denotes liability of a state for conduct which is in breach of international law and which causes injury to another state or that state's nationals. Responsibility refers to the responsibility of one state to another for the non-observance of the obligations imposed by the international legal system. The International Law Commission (ILC) produced *Draft Articles on Responsibility of States for Internationally Wrongful Acts 2001* (Draft articles) and the General Assembly Resolution 56/83 December 12, 2001, recommended the text of these Draft articles to governments for adoption.

The General Commentary to the Draft Articles 2001 states that the Draft articles:

> "seek to formulate, by way of codification and progressive development, the basic rules of international law concerning the responsibility of States for internationally wrongful acts".

The emphasis of the Draft articles is on the secondary rules of responsibility.

They are set out as follows:

- Part 1, the Internationally Wrongful Act of a State;
- Part 2, content of the International Responsibility of a State;
- Part 3, the Implementation of the International Responsibility of a State; and
- Part 4 deals with the general provisions applicable to the Articles as a whole.

Note that all references to Draft articles below are to the *Draft Articles on Responsibility of States for Internationally Wrongful Acts 2001* unless otherwise stated.

BASIC RULES

Draft art.1 maintains, "Every internationally wrongful act of a State entails the international responsibility of that State".

Draft art.2 provides:

> "There is an internationally wrongful act of a State when conduct consisting of an action or omission:
> (a) is attributable to the State under international law; and
> (b) constitutes a breach of an international obligation of the State",

i.e., there must be an act attributable to a state and a breach of an international obligation must have occurred.

Draft art.1 reflects customary international law, namely when a state commits an internationally wrongful act against another state international responsibility is established, "immediately as between the two States", see *Chorzow Factory (Indemnity) case (Merits)* (1928) (see above, p.23); see also *Corfu Channel case (Merits)* (1949) (see above, p.75).

"Refusal to fulfil a treaty obligation involves international responsibility", *Interpretation of Peace Treaties with Bulgaria, Hungary and Romania (Second Phase)* (1950) I.C.J. Rep. 221 and in the *Rainbow Warrior case (New Zealand/France)* (1990) R.I.A.A. Volume XX 317 it was emphasised that, "any violation by a State of any obligation, of whatever origin, gives rise to State responsibility."

Note, internationally wrongful acts are determined by international law and not domestic law:

> "The characterization of an act of a State as internationally wrongful is governed by international law. Such characterization is not affected by the characterization of the same act as lawful by internal use", Draft art.3.

The origin of the act, e.g. criminal, tortuous etc. is not significant:

> "There is a breach of an international obligation by a State when an act of that State is not in conformity with what is required of it by that obligation regardless of its origin or character", Draft art.12.

See also *the Rainbow Warrior case (above)*. However the state must be under an obligation at the time the act occurred, Draft art.13. Otherwise an act of a state does not constitute a breach of an international obligation. According to J. Crawford, 'International Law Commission's Articles on State Responsibility— Introduction, Text and Commentaries', (Cambridge, 2002), p.131, Draft art.13:

> "provides an important guarantee for States in terms of claims of responsibility. Its formulation ("does not constitute ... unless ...") it is in keeping with the idea of a guarantee against the retrospective application of international law in matters of State responsibility."

However note that once responsibility has been established the subsequent termination of the obligation does not affect the responsibility, e.g. see *Rainbow Warrior case* (see above, p.84) in which it was held France's responsibility for its earlier breach remained although the passage of time had terminated the treaty obligation.

Liability is incurred if a state is implicated in the wrongful acts of another state:

> "a State which aids or assists in the commission of an internationally wrongful act by the latter is internationally responsibility for doing so if: (a) that State does so with knowledge of the circumstances of the internationally wrongful act; and (b) the act would be internationally wrongful if committed by that State", Draft art.16.

In the same circumstances a state which directs and controls another state in the commission of an internationally wrongful act by the latter will be held internationally responsible, Draft art.17.

Recognised defence pleas, which may be utilised by a state to deny responsibility, are:

- Consent (Draft art.20);
- Self-defence (Draft art.21);
- Counter measures (Draft art.22);
- Force majeure (an act which cannot be anticipated, an "act of God") (Draft art.23);
- Distress (Draft art.24); and
- Necessity (Draft art.25).

Provisions or omissions of domestic law are not an accepted defence, see *Free Zones of Upper Savoy and the District of Gex* (1932) PCIJ Rep Ser A/B, No 46 and Draft art.3 (see above, p.84).

Fault/strict liability

As to whether state responsibility is absolute or depends upon fault being demonstrated, there is evidence in customary international law to support both. The *Home Missionary Society Claim* (1920) 6 R.I.A.A. 42 and *Corfu Channel case (Merits)* (see above, p.75) 1949 point in favour of fault liability whereas the *Caire Claim* (1929) 5 R.I.A.A. 516 comes down in favour of absolute liability.

Today fault liability is too complicated to apply and, increasingly, strict liability is favoured. However it should be noted the behaviour of the claimant state may be taken into consideration in assessing the reparation payable. Draft art.39 provides:

> "In the determination of reparation, account shall be taken of the contribution to the injury by wilfull or negligent action or omission of the injured State or any person or entity in relation to whom reparation is sought."

In the *LaGrand case (Germany v United States)* (2001) 40 I.L.M. 1069 the ICJ recognised, "that Germany may be criticised for the manner in which these proceedings were filed and for their timing." This referred to Germany's delay in claiming a breach had occurred and, thus, the delay in instituting proceedings.

Imputability

Imputability in state responsibility means "attributable". State responsibility may be attributed to any state organ and any entity authorised to exercise governmental authority, even if the authority is exceeded or the entity acted contrary to instructions, Draft arts 4, 5 and 7.

The basic rule is set out in Draft art.4:

> "(1) the conduct of any State organ shall be considered an act of that State under international law, whether the organ exercises legislative, executive, judicial or any other functions, whatever position it holds in the organisation of the State, and whatever its character as an organ of the central government or of a territorial unit of the State.
>
> (2) An organ includes any person or entity which has that status in accordance with the internal law of the State."

Draft art.5 is concerned with the attribution to the state of conduct by entities, which are not state organs within the terms of Draft art.4, but are, nevertheless, authorised to exercise governmental authority. What is important is that the entity in question is empowered by the state to exercise elements of governmental authority and that the entity in question was acting in that capacity at the time of the alleged breach.

An entity covered by Draft arts 4 and 5 acting pursuant to governmental authority will be attributed to the state, even if authority has been exceeded or instructions have been contravened, Draft art.7.

State control

Conduct not of a state organ or entity, but attributed to a state in international law, is dealt with in Draft arts 8–11.

Draft art.8 addresses the issue of private persons following state instructions in carrying out the wrongful conduct and also with instances of private persons acting under the state's direction or control. Draft art.8 provides:

> "The conduct of a person or group of persons shall be considered an act of a State under international law if the person or group of persons is in fact acting on the instructions of, or under the direction and control of, that State in carrying out the conduct."

The level of control required for the attribution of state responsibility demands that the offending conduct be integral and not merely incidental or peripheral.

▮ DEFINITION CHECKPOINT
Control The standard of control required for attribution is not settled. Two often quoted standards referred to are "effective control" and "overall control".

In *Nicaragua v USA (Merits) (Military and Paramilitary Activities in and against Nicaragua)* (1986) I.C.J. 14, the question being addressed was whether the conduct of the Contras' could be attributed to the US, thus making the US responsible for the Contras breaches of international humanitarian law. Although the Court, following an analysis of "control" held the US responsible for "planning, direction and support" afforded to the Contras, it nevertheless denied that all the conduct of the Contras could be attributed to the US. The Court stated for such conduct:

> "to give rise to legal responsibility of the United States, it would in principle have to be proved that the state had *effective control*

of the military or paramilitary operations in the course of which the alleged violations were committed".

In the *Tadic case* (1999) 38 I.L.M. 1518, the Appeals Chamber of the International Criminal Tribunal for the Former Yugoslavia emphasised:

"The requirements of international law for the attribution to States of acts performed by private individuals, is that the State exercise control over the individuals the *degree of control* may, however, vary according to the factual circumstances of each case. The Appeals Chamber fails to see why in each and every circumstance international law should require a high threshold for the test of control."

In that case the Appeals Chamber was seeking to establish the control required over armed forces by the Yugoslavian authorities to characterise the armed conflict as international. The Appeals Chamber held the necessary control was:

"*overall control* going beyond the mere financing and equipping of such forces and involving also participation in the planning and supervision of military operations".

Note, the legal issues and factual situations in the two cases were different and in *Tadić* (above) the Appeal Chamber was addressing the issue of individual criminal responsibility rather than that of state responsibility as well as the rules of international humanitarian law applicable.

The control necessary for conduct to be attributed is determined on a case by case basis.

Draft art.9 concerns the relatively rare case of conduct carried out in the absence or default of the official authorities.

Draft art.10 provides that the conduct of an insurrectional movement which becomes the new government of a state shall be considered an act of that state under international law.

Consequences of incurring responsibility

The obligation on the offending state is to cease the wrongful conduct and to offer appropriate assurances and guarantees of non-repetition, if circumstances so require, Draft art.30.

Draft art.31 reflects the customary international law obligation for the offending state to make full reparation for the injury caused by the internationally wrongful act. "Injury" is defined as including any damage, whether material or moral, caused by the internationally wrongful act of a state.

The customary international law is that as stated in the *Chorzow Factory case (Jurisdiction)* (1927) (see above, p.23), in that:

> "It is a principle of international law that the breach of an engagement involves an obligation to make reparation in an adequate form. Reparation therefore is the indispensable compliment of a failure to apply convention and there is no necessity for this to be stated in the convention itself."

Reparation

The aim of reparation is to restore previous conditions and, if this is not possible, then to give compensation, either in kind or with money.

KEY CASE

THE CHORZOW FACTORY (INDEMNITY) CASE (1928) (MERITS) (SEE ABOVE, P.23):

> "The essential principle ...—a principle which seems to be established by international practice and in particular by the decisions of arbitral tribunals—is that reparation must, so far as possible, wipe out all the consequences of the illegal act and re-establish the situation which would, in all probability, have existed if that act had not been committed. Restitution in kind, or, if this is not possible, payment of a sum corresponding to the value which a restitution in kind would bear; the award, if need be, of damages for loss sustained which would not be covered by restitution in kind or payment in place of it—such are the principles which should serve to determine the amount of compensation due for an act contrary to international law."

Forms of reparation

Forms of reparation can be found in Draft art.34, which provides:

> " ... full reparation for the injury caused by the internationally wrongful act shall take the form of restitution, compensation and satisfaction, either singly or in combination ... "

Restitution in kind is rare, however, see the *Martini case (Italy v Venezuela)*

(1930) 2 R.I.A.A. 975, 1002 and the *Temple case* (1962) I.C.J. Rep. 6 for instances of such an order being made.

See also Draft art.35 which spells out the obligation to make restitution:

> "Provided and to the extent that restitution:
> (a) is not materially impossible;
> (b) does not involve a burden out of all proportion to the benefit deriving from restitution instead of compensation."

Monetary compensation is more common. The rules regarding monetary compensation were spelt out in the *Chorzow Factory (Indemnity)* case *(Merits)* (see above, p.23). See also Draft art.31 (see above, p.88) and Draft art.36(1), which provides:

> "The State responsible for an internationally wrongful act is under an obligation to compensate for the damage caused thereby, in so far as such damage is not made good by restitution. (2) The compensation shall cover any financially assessable damage including loss of profits in so far as it is established."

The Commentary to Draft art.36 provides that "financially assessable" is intended to exclude compensation for "moral damage" to a state. (J. Crawford (see above, p.85), at 218)

Satisfaction for non-material loss, in certain circumstances satisfaction may be fulfilled by acknowledgement of the breach, an expression of regret or, a formal apology, Draft art.37.

Exemplary or punitive damages: there is a reluctance to award such damages, however see the *I'm Alone case (Canada v United States)* 3 R.I.A.A. 1609 (1933/35); (1935) 29 A.J.I.L. 326, in which it was recommended the US should pay the Canadian government US $25,000, "as a material amend in respect of the wrong". It was further recommended the US should pay certain sums in respect of benefits for those crew members who were not implicated in smuggling the liquor into the US. Interest may be awarded in some cases and as a general principle may be paid on the principal sum representing the loss sustained by the victim state. Payment may be necessary if, for instance, the sum to be paid has been quantified at a date earlier than the date of settlement. Draft art.38(1) provides for the payment of interest and prescribes that the interest rate and method of calculation is to be set so as to achieve full reparation. Draft art.38(2) provides that interest:

> "runs from the date when the principal sum should have been paid until the date the obligation to pay is fulfilled."

DEFINITION CHECKPOINT

Erga omnes norms/obligations
Obligations owed to the international legal community as a whole and obligations which every state has an interest in having respected.

The issue of obligations *erga omnes* was dealt with by the ICJ in the *Barcelona Traction case* (1970) (see above, p.9). The ICJ in that case distinguished between obligations owed by a state towards the international community as a whole and those obligations arising between states. The ICJ stated:

> "By their very nature the former are the concern of all states. In view of the importance of the rights involved, all states can be held to have a legal interest in their protection; they are obligations *erga omnes.*"

Such obligations, the ICJ stated, were derived from, "the outlawing of acts of aggression, and of genocide ... " and from, "rules concerning the basic rights of the human person, including protection from slavery and racial discrimination."

In the *East Timor case (Portugal v Australia)* (1995) I.C.J. Rep. 90, the ICJ endorsed the Portuguese claim that self-determination, "as it evolved from the Charter and from UN practice" had an *erga omnes* character as being "irreproachable". The notion of an obligation *erga omnes* is closely akin to the acknowledgement of certain norms as peremptory, see for example arts 53 and 64 of Vienna Convention on the Law of Treaties.

The term "peremptory" is used in Draft art.40 wherein it is stated that international responsibility will be entailed, "by a serious breach by a state of an obligation arising under a peremptory norm of general international law." "A breach of such an obligation is deemed to be serious if it involves a gross or systematic failure by the responsible state to fulfil the obligation", Draft art.40(2).

The Draft articles do not provide any examples of peremptory norms, although the Commentary to the Draft articles makes reference to the prohibition of aggression, slavery, genocide, racial discrimination, torture, apartheid and the right of self-determination. Draft art.41 calls for co-operation amongst states to bring an end through lawful means any serious breach, within the meaning of Draft art.40. Draft art.41(2) provides that states are under an obligation to refrain from recognising as lawful situations created by serious breaches within the meaning of Draft art.40 and to refrain from providing aid or assistance in the maintenance of the situation.

Draft art.42 deals with the entitlement of the injured state to invoke the responsibility of another state if the obligation breached is owed to:

"(a) that State individually; or

(b) a group of states including that state, or the international community as a whole, and the breach of the obligation

(i) specially affects that state; or

(ii) is of such a character as radically to change the position of all the other states to which the obligation is owed with respect to the further performance of the obligation."

Draft art.43 deals with way in which the injured state shall intimate notice of its claim to the responsible state.

DIPLOMATIC PROTECTION

CLAIMS ON BEHALF OF INDIVIDUALS: THE NATIONALITY OF CLAIMS RULE

A state may bring a claim of diplomatic protection against another state on the grounds that one of its nationals has suffered a wrong at the hands of a host state.

In 2006, the ILC adopted a set of Draft Articles on Diplomatic Protection, which represent both codification and progressive development of the law.

Only the state of nationality may bring a claim on behalf of one of its nationals against another state, Draft art.3, Draft Articles on Diplomatic Protection 2006.

An individual:

- cannot force a state to bring a claim, see Draft arts 2, 19(a) and (b) Draft Articles on Diplomatic Protection 2006;
- cannot prevent a state from exercising diplomatic protection as attempted *per* the Calvo Clause (see *below*), (see Draft art.2, 19(a) and (b) Draft Articles on Diplomatic Protection 2006; and
- States do not act as agents of the individual and any damages received can be withheld by the state (see *Civilian War Claimants Association v The King* [1932] (see above, p.49); however see also, Draft art.19(c) Draft Articles on Diplomatic Protection).

Calvo Clause

Named after Carlos Calvo, a nineteenth-century Argentinean jurist, the Calvo Clause was frequently inserted in contracts involving Latin American countries and US citizens, whereby the latter undertook in the event of a dispute not to invoke the diplomatic protection of the US but rather agreed to be subject to the local courts. However in the *North American Dredging Company* case 4 (1926) R.I.A.A. 26 it was held that " ... an alien ... cannot deprive the government of his nation of its undoubted right of applying international remedies to violations of international law committed to his damage."

A state, in pursuing a claim on behalf of an individual, is exercising its own right as a state, the sole claimant to the international stage, see *Mavromatis Palestine Concessions case* (1924) P.C.I.J. Rep. Ser. A No. 2 12, in which it was stated:

> "Once a State has taken up a case on behalf of one of its subjects before an international tribunal, in the eyes of the latter the State is sole claimant."

The matter of nationality and who is a national is determined by the domestic law of the State (see Draft art.4 Draft Articles on Diplomatic Protection 2006). International law provides no definition of nationality. However the ICJ has stated that for diplomatic protection to be afforded there must be a genuine link between the individual and the state alleging nationality, see *Nottebohm case* (1955) I.C.J. Rep. 4, in which Guatemala challenged Liechtenstein's claim on behalf of an individual who, after a few weeks in Liechtenstein, became a Liechtenstein citizen. The ICJ, at 23, described nationality as:

> "A legal bond having, as its basis a social fact of attachment, a genuine connection of existence, interests and sentiments, together with the existence of reciprocal rights and duties".

As a rule, a state will only take up a claim on behalf of a person who is a national at the time of injury and a national at the time the claim is being presented (see Draft art.5 Draft Articles on Diplomatic Protection 2006).

In the case of dual nationality one national state will not normally take up a claim against another national state. In bringing a claim against a third state, the favoured approach is that both national states act together, see however *Merge Claim case* (1955) 22 I.L.R. 443 (the state with which the individual has the closest connection); *Salem case* (1932) 2 R.I.A.A. 1161 (both states); *Iran—US* No. A/18 (1984) 5 Iran—USCTR 251 (the "dominant and effective nationality" test); see also Draft arts 5 and 6 of ILC Draft Articles on Diplomatic Protection 2006.

Traditionally, a state that injured a stateless person could not be held internationally responsible, nor was any state competent to raise a claim on a stateless person's behalf. However, Draft art.8 of the Draft Articles on Diplomatic Protection 2006, which represents an element of progressive development of the law, maintains that states *may* exercise diplomatic protection over stateless persons and refugees who at the date of injury and the date of presentation of the claim are "lawfully and habitually resident in that state".

CLAIMS ON BEHALF OF COMPANIES/SHAREHOLDERS

In the *Barcelona Traction case* (see above, p.9) at 42 it was held that, "no absolute test of the "genuine connection" has found general acceptance". Here the ICJ maintained the company's state of nationality has the right to bring the claim, even when the company operates outside that state and the shareholders are non-nationals. The ICJ was of the view that, since the company was still in existence, the option of bringing a claim on behalf of the company remained with the state of nationality (in this case Canada.) The ICJ denied diplomatic protection for the shareholders on the basis this would lead to confusion, given shares are "widely scattered and frequently change hands" at 49. However, if a company ceases to exist the ICJ held the shareholders' state of nationality could initiate a claim for injuries sustained.

In the *Case Concerning Ahmadou Sadio Diallo (Republic of Guinea v Democratic Republic of Congo) (Preliminary Objections)*, ICJ 2007, the ICJ held that no "substitution doctrine"—i.e. that the state of nationality of the company may be substituted by the state of nationality of the shareholders— is recognised in customary international law. However, Draft art.9 of the Draft Articles on Diplomatic Protection 2006 provides:

> "... the State of nationality means the State under whose law the corporation was incorporated. However, when the corporation is controlled by nationals of another State or States and has no substantial business activities in the State of incorporation, and the seat of management and the financial control of the corporation are both located in another State, that State shall be regarded as the State of nationality".

Article 12 goes on to lay down a general prohibition against the state of nationality of shareholders exercising diplomatic protection, except where the corporation has ceased to exist in the state of incorporation or where the corporation was injured by the state of which it was a national.

As with individuals, a state is able to exercise diplomatic protection over a corporation when it was a national of that state, both at the time of injury and presentation of claim, Draft art.11 Draft Articles on Diplomatic Protection 2006.

For the position of the UK see Rules Regarding International Claims issued by the British Foreign and Commonwealth Office 1985. These reflect established international law and, e.g. with regard to companies reflect the *Barcelona Traction case* (see above, p.9).

EXHAUSTION OF LOCAL REMEDIES

This is a basic rule of international law and is reflected in Draft art.44(b) of ILC Draft Articles on State Responsibility 2001. Draft art.44(b) provides:

> "The responsibility of a State may not be invoked if the claim is one to which the rule of exhaustion of local remedies applies and any available and effective local remedy has not been exhausted."

The exhaustion of local remedies is required to:

- provide alleged offending states with the opportunity to afford redress;
- minimise the number of international claims; and
- protect state sovereignty.

DEFINITION CHECKPOINT
Local remedies
This term encompasses not just courts but "tribunals ... the use of the procedural facilities which domestic law makes available to litigants before such courts and tribunals. It is the whole system of legal protection, as provided by domestic law ... " (*Ambatieios Arbitration* (1956) 12 R.I.A.A. 83).

It is important that all administrative, arbitral or judicial remedies are pursued. However, only effective remedies must be exhausted. Also, exhaustion of remedies is not necessary where:

- there is no justice to exhaust;

- efforts to obtain redress would be obstructed;
- it is expressed explicitly in a treaty; and
- in the event of direct injury by one state against another.

Draft arts 14 and 15 of the Draft Articles on Diplomatic Protection 2006 also require the exhaustion of local remedies and stipulate exceptions to this rule respectively.

TREATMENT OF NATIONALS/STANDARD OF TREATMENT

Each state has an obligation to protect nationals from another state who are lawfully within its territory. If they fail in this obligation responsibility is incurred. However what treatment should such individuals be afforded?

The National Treatment Standard
According to this standard, non-nationals are to be accorded the same treatment as host state nationals. See Resolution 40/144 (1985) Declaration on the Human Rights of Individuals who are not Nationals of the Country in Which They Live (United Nations).

The International Minimum Standard
This standard is ill-defined but is held to be breached when the offending conduct falls so short "that every reasonable and impartial man would readily recognize its insufficiency" *Neer Claim* (1926) 4 R.I.A.A. 60.

However, the emergence and development of international human rights law, particularly since 1948, has afforded greater protection for individuals and has also exposed states to external review.

Note, Article 32 of the 1951 Geneva Convention on the Status relating to Refugees precludes expulsion of a refugee lawfully in the territory of a contracting State except on grounds of national security or public order and art.33 prohibits expulsion or return of a refugee to a territory where his life or freedom would be threatened on account of his race, religion, nationality, membership of a particular social group or political opinion (the principle of *non-refoulement*). See also art.3 of the UN Convention against Torture and other Cruel, Inhuman or Degrading Treatment or Punishment 1984.

The state of nationality is required to receive a national expelled from another state unless a third state is willing to admit the individual and the individual is willing to go to the third state.

EXPROPRIATION OF THE PROPERTY OF ALIENS

Expropriation may be defined as the compulsory taking of private property by the state including unreasonable interference with the use, enjoyment, or disposal of property, Draft art.10(3)(a) 1961 Harvard Draft Convention. Property includes:

> "All moveable and immovable property, whether tangible or intangible, including industrial, literary and artistic property, as well as rights and interests in any property",

Draft art.10(7) 1961 Harvard Draft Convention) and now includes contractual rights, see, e.g. *Starrett Housing Corp. v Iran* (Interlocutory Award) 4 Iran-USCTR 122; (1984) 23 I.L.M. 1090; *Amoco International Finance Corporation v Iran* 15 Iran-USCTR 189; (1986) 82 A.J.I.L. 358.

Denial of effective use of private property through fiscal and regulatory measures is described as "creeping", "constructive" or indirect expropriation, see *Starrett Housing Corp. v Iran (above).*

The criteria used for expropriation to be deemed as lawful have divided developed capital investing states from that of developing states. The stance of the former is reflected in Resolution 1803/17 (1962) Permanent Sovereignty over Natural Resources (United Nations) and this is seen as reflecting customary international law. Paragraph four of Resolution 1803/17 (1962) maintains where nationalisation, expropriation or requisitioning is necessary for public utility, security or national interest, it should be non-discriminatory and involve compensation determined by the rules in force in the expropriating state and international law.

Public purpose has played little role in consideration of whether expropriation was lawful, see *Liamco case* (1981) 20 I.L.M.

Non-discrimination has likewise played a minimal role in consideration of whether expropriation was lawful and in the *Amoco International Finance Corporation v Iran* (above) it was acknowledged that an element of discrimination may in certain circumstances be tolerated, such as being reasonably related to the public purpose.

Compensation has been the predominant feature in assessing lawfulness or otherwise of expropriation. For compensation to conform to the international law standard it must be prompt, adequate and effective, as per US Secretary of State Hull's 1940 statement contained in a letter to the Mexican Government on the issue of Mexico's expropriation of foreign oil interests. The term "appropriate compensation" is also used in Resolution 1803/17 (*above*), and appropriate is interpreted as prompt, adequate and effective. This "appropriate compensation" should be assessed on a case by case basis but it is accepted that compensation is given for the monetary value of the property with some account being given to future profit lost, see *Amco Asia Corporation v the Republic of Indonesia* (1985) 24 I.L.M. 1022.

Compensation should be paid in a readily convertible currency and, if payment is deferred, interest must be paid.

The position of developing states is reflected in art.2(c) of the Charter of Economic Rights and Duties of States 1974 (the 1974 Charter). Namely compensation, if paid, will take into account the relevant laws and regulations and circumstances considered pertinent by the expropriating state. Any dispute over compensation is to be decided, unless otherwise agreed, by the domestic law of the "taking" state. The 1974 Charter is not regarded as customary international law, see *Texaco case* (1978) 53 I.L.R. (1977); 17 I.L.M. (1978).

Note, it is necessary to distinguish between lawful and unlawful expropriation, "since the rules applicable to the compensation to be paid by the expropriating state differ according to the legal characterisation of the taking", *Amoco case* (see above, p.97) at 246. Unlawful expropriation warrants full restitution in kind or the equivalent monetary value with the possibility in some instances for account to be taken of loss or expected loss of profits. This differs from lawful expropriation which only warrants compensation reflecting the value of the property at the time of takeover.

Settlement of Disputes

Today, capital investing and importing states deal with the possibility of expropriation by way of bi-lateral treaties which contain provisions for compensation. Settlement may also be effected by negotiation and "lump-sum settlement" agreements.

International bodies have been established with jurisdiction over claims, e.g. US/Iran Tribunal 1981; and UN Claims Commission 1991 in respect of war claims against Iraq. See also 1965 Convention on the Settlement of Investment Disputes between States and Nationals of other states, which provides a mechanism for the settlement of disputes between contracting parties and companies of and companies possessing the nationality of a contracting party.

STATE RESPONSIBILITY TOWARDS THE ENVIRONMENT

Historically, rules of state responsibility were employed to provide redress for environmental damage. The rules in question were those which had evolved under customary international law.

THE TRAIL SMELTER ARBITRATION 3 R.I.A.A. 1905 (1938/41)

In this case it was acknowledged that that there exists a general principle of international law—and in this case US law—that no state has the right to:

" ... use or permit the use of its territory in such a manner as to cause injury by fumes in or to the territory of another or the properties or persons therein, when the cause is of serious consequences and the injury is established by clear and convincing evidence."

In this particular case the damage had been caused by the emission of sulphur dioxide from a smelter plant at Trail, ten miles on the Canadian side of the US/Canadian border. The damage was sustained in Washington State.

See also the *Gut Dam Arbitration* (1969) 8 I.L.M. 118 and the *Corfu Channel (Merits) case* (see above, p.75), where it was acknowledged there is a responsibility on every state, "not to allow knowingly its territory to be used for acts contrary to the rights of other states."

This customary international law was endorsed in Principle 21, adopted at Stockholm in 1972, as placing on states an obligation to ensure that activities within their jurisdictional control do not cause damage to the environment of other states or of areas beyond the limits of national jurisdiction. This is now reflected in Principle 2 of the Rio Declaration, adopted on June 14, 1992, following the UN Conference on Environment and Development held in Rio de Janeiro. However, since the 1970s environmental issues have been addressed more frequently by way of the "precautionary principle".

The principal characteristic of international environmental instruments over the last forty years has been the focus on co-operation. There are a large number of instruments dealing with the protection of the environment. These instruments range from dealing with certain hazards, which are now recognised as producing adverse affects on the environment to those, which deal with specific areas such as the marine environment.

The Conference in Rio de Janeiro on the Environment and Development (UNCED) acknowledged there were a number of environmental problems, which now required to be addressed by way of co-operation between states. Of particular significance was the conference's endorsement of the concept of sustainable development. Sustainable development may be defined as meeting the needs of the present generation without compromising the ability of future generations to do the same. See also the Bruntland Report of the World Commission on Environment and Development (WCED) 1987. The emphasis throughout the Rio Declaration is on co-operation the obligation on states to take precautionary measures and also recognition is given to the "polluter pays principal" and environmental impact assessments. States are also under an obligation to engage in consultation in circumstances where there is a risk of trans-boundary pollution. States are also required to notify the international community of any emergencies.

In addition to the Declaration, Agenda 21 was adopted, namely a programme of action as well as a Convention on Biological Diversity, a Convention on Climate Change and a Statement of Principles on Forests. In 1992 the Commission on Sustainable Development was established to monitor the progress of implementing the contents of Agenda 21. Agenda 21 has no binding legal effect but is regarded as setting out a plan of action for the international community.

A follow up meeting was held in Johannesburg, South Africa, namely the World Summit on Sustainable Development, 2002. The international community has also looked at global warming, the impact of the depletion of the ozone layer and, e.g. the disposal of hazardous waste and the control of nuclear activity.

International environmental law is now a highly specialised area and the numerous international instruments include:

- 1979 Convention on Long-range Trans-boundary Air Pollution and eight subsequent Protocols all of which are in force;
- 1985 Vienna Convention on the Protection of the Ozone Layer, subsequently supplemented by the 1987 Montreal Protocol on Substances that Deplete the Ozone Layer and the 1989 Helsinki Declaration on the Protection of the Ozone Layer;
- 1991 UN Convention on Environmental Impact Assessment.

This package is designed to promote co-operation, scientific research and information exchange, while the Protocols regulate the consumption of chloroflurocarbons by setting a maximum consumption level and prescribing a freeze on halons.

The Framework Convention on Climate Change 1992 was designed to stabilise greenhouse gas concentrations in the atmosphere. This was followed by the Kyoto Protocol 1997 and further amended by the Marrakech Accords and Declaration 2001. Subsequent attempts to achieve legally binding restrictions on carbon emissions have, to date, proved unsuccessful.

Regarding the transfer of hazardous waste the applicable instrument is the 1989 Basque Convention on the Control of Trans-boundary Movement of

Hazardous waste and their Disposal and the subsequent Protocol on Liability and Compensation for Damage Resulting from Trans-boundary Movement of Hazardous waste and their Disposal.

The instruments in respect of regulating nuclear activity include:

- 1963 Treaty Banning Nuclear Weapon Tests in Outer Space and Under Water;
- 1986 The Vienna Convention on the Early Notification of a Nuclear Accident;
- 1986 Convention on Assistance in the Case of a Nuclear Accident or Radiological Emergency; and
- 1994 Convention on Nuclear Safety.

There are also a number of Conventions, which relate to protection of the environment even during the course of hostilities.

Note the Advisory Opinion of the ICJ in the *Legality of the Threat or Use of Nuclear Weapons* (1997) 35 I.L.M. 809 and 1343, which stated it is "contrary to the rules of international law applicable in armed conflict" to use or threaten to use nuclear weapons. A principle emerging from that case was the recognition that states are under a customary obligation to negotiate in good faith for nuclear disarmament.

Note also the ILC Draft articles on Prevention of Trans-boundary Harm from Hazardous Activities 2001, which deal with activities not prohibited by international law but which involve a risk of causing significant trans-boundary harm through their physical consequences, Draft art.1. These are only designed to apply in the event of a significant harm being likely in the territory of another state.

Revision Checklist

You should now know and understand:

- **The definition of state responsibility;**
- **The legal regime that applies to state responsibility;**
- **The rules used to determine internationally wrongful acts;**
- **The defence pleas which may be invoked by a state to deny responsibility;**
- **The aim of reparation;**

- The importance of the *Chorzow Factory (Indemnity) (Merits) case* to the law of state responsibility;

- The definition of obligations *erga omnes*;

- The importance of the *Barcelona Traction case* in relation to obligations *erga omnes*;

- The role and substance of the ILC Draft Articles on Diplomatic Protection 2006;

- The importance of nationality of claims rule;

- The requirement to exhaust local remedies, and the exceptions thereto;

- The meaning of the international minimum standard;

- The position of shareholders in relation to diplomatic protection claims over corporations;

- The criteria used to determine lawful expropriation;

- The positions taken by developing and developed states with regard to compensation for expropriation;

- The way in which most expropriation disputes are now settled.

QUESTION AND ANSWER

The Question

"... an alien ... cannot deprive the government of his nation of its undoubted right of applying international remedies to violations of international law committed to his damage", (*North American Dredging Company case (US/Mexico)* (1926) 4. R.I.A.A. 26 at 29.

Discuss in the context of the nationality of claims rule and state responsibility.

Advice and the Answer

This answer should address what is the nationality of claims rule. It should highlight the importance of nationality as a sovereign right of the state and its importance in the context of state responsibility and diplomatic protection. The answer may also make reference to how nationality is acquired and how it lies within the prerogative of the state. It is important to emphasise that the nationality of claims rule reinforces the primacy of the state and relate this to the quotation cited in the question.

The Question (2)

The problems of the environment confronting the international community are such that they can no longer be dealt with effectively through the principle of state responsibility.

Evaluate and discuss.

Advice and the Answer

Initially the answer should address the way in which state responsibility was invoked and employed with reference being made to the *Trail Smelter* case and the *Gut Dam* case. The strengths and weaknesses of dealing with the environment by way of state responsibility may be discussed. Alternative approaches, e.g. the precautionary approach should then be examined with reference to relevant international instruments.

State Jurisdiction

10

INTRODUCTION

The exercise of jurisdiction refers to the power of the state under international law to govern persons and property by its domestic law (criminal/civil) and denotes jurisdiction to prescribe, proscribe, adjudicate and enforce.

The exercise or non-exercise of jurisdiction is regulated by a state's domestic law and there is no requirement a state exercises jurisdiction in given circumstances. In some circumstances more than one state may have a claim to exercise jurisdiction.

What the international legal system demands is that there be a tangible link between the individual over whom jurisdiction is exercised and/or the forum of the incident and the state exercising jurisdiction.

See the *Lotus case* (1927) P.C.I.J. Ser. A No.10, in which the discretion enjoyed by a state was acknowledged as existing to the extent that, unless there was a prohibition on the exercise of state jurisdiction, jurisdiction could be exercised.

The principal bases of jurisdiction are:
   (a) territorial principle;
   (b) nationality principle;
   (c) protective (or security) principle;
   (d) universality principle; and
   (e) passive personality principle.

(a)–(d) are found in the Harvard Research Draft Convention on Jurisdiction with Respect to Crime 1935, which was the culmination of work examining state practice. As a Draft the Convention was not binding but was regarded as reflecting what was established as customary international law.
   (e) was not adopted by the Harvard Draft Convention.

The territorial principle is the most common basis for the exercise of jurisdiction.

THE TERRITORIAL PRINCIPLE

> **DEFINITION CHECKPOINT**
>
> *Territorial Principle*
> Can be:
> - *subjective* territorial principle—exercised by the state in which the offence is allegedly initiated
> - *objective* territorial principle—exercised by the State in which the offence completed.

These principles acknowledge that an offence is not necessarily initiated and fulfilled in the one territory. The traditional example given is that of a person standing on one side of a national border firing a gun and injuring a person on the other side of the border. The state in which the person shot the gun from has jurisdiction on the basis of the subjective territorial principle, and the state in which the injury was sustained has jurisdiction under the objective territorial principle. In respect of such offences both states can claim jurisdiction. The one which will exercise jurisdiction will be determined by factors such as which state has custody of the alleged offender. Practical factors determine which state exercises jurisdiction and there is no hierarchy of legal precedence.

Certain crimes prompted an extension of territorial jurisdiction beyond the geographical territory of the state, e.g. as witnessed in the response of certain countries to dealing with the child sex industry. See also jurisdiction based on the "effects principle", e.g. the anti-trust legislation of the US.

The territorial sea is the belt of sea adjacent to the coast over which the coastal state enjoys sovereignty. This extends to the airspace above the territorial sea as well as its bed and subsoil, see arts 1 and 2 of the Geneva Convention on the Territorial Sea and the Contiguous Zone 1958 and art.1 and 2 of the Convention on the Law of the Sea 1982. It extends to a limit not exceeding 12 nautical miles, art.3 of 1982 Convention (*above*).

Note, the right of innocent passage is recognised through territorial sea and the coastal state may take steps necessary to halt passage which is not innocent, as stated in art.16 of the 1958 Convention and art.25 of the 1982 Convention.

A coastal state's criminal jurisdiction is limited to certain defined circumstances, e.g. where the consequences of the crime extend to the coastal state. A coastal state's civil jurisdiction is strictly limited, e.g. as to when the vessel is passing through territorial waters after having left internal waters, art.20 of the 1958 Convention and art.28 of the 1982 Convention).

Foreign warships may be required to leave the territorial sea immediately. Art.23 of 1958 Convention and art.30 of 1982 Convention address the issue of hot pursuit, laying down the conditions under which the coastal state may pursue a vessel leaving its territorial waters when the vessel is suspected of having breached the pursuing state's laws and regulations. See also Ch.8 for further discussion on the law of the sea.

THE NATIONALITY PRINCIPLE

Jurisdiction is exercised under this principle because of the offender's nationality. The nationality principle has been used more frequently in civil law countries than common law countries. Common law countries have tended to restrict the application of the nationality principle to what is regarded as the most serious principles, e.g. the UK Officials Secrets Act 1989.

THE PROTECTIVE (OR SECURITY) PRINCIPLE

Jurisdiction is exercised under this principle because of a threat to state security through the commission of an act by a non-national abroad, see *Joyce v D.P.P.* [1946] A.C. 347 (HL) (Lord Haw Haw). Joyce was convicted of treason for the broadcast of Nazi propaganda to Britain from Germany during the Second World War.

In the case of *AG of Israel v Eichmann* [1961] 36 I.L.R. 5, the protective security principle was employed in conjunction with the universality principle.

THE UNIVERSALITY PRINCIPLE

The exercise of the universality principle is precipitated by the type of offence allegedly committed. The crime in question is contrary to, and prohibited by, international law. Any state may exercise jurisdiction on the basis of the universality principle, however the state must be in possession of the alleged offender. See *AG of Israel v Eichmann* [1961] *(above)* and *Congo v Belgium* (2002) I.C.J. Rep. 3, *The Case Concerning the Arrest Warrant*.

International crimes
Piracy under customary international law is the true international offence, see art.19 1958 Geneva Convention on the High Seas; and art.101 1982 Convention on the Law of the Sea.

Other acts subject to universal jurisdiction are war crimes, crimes against peace, and crimes against humanity, see the International Military Tribunal, art.6; International Criminal Tribunal for the Former Yugoslavia, Statute art.5; International Criminal Tribunal for Rwanda, Statute art.3; Statute of International Criminal Court art.5; and the Draft Code of Crimes Against Peace and Security of Mankind 1996.

For quasi-international crimes, jurisdiction is established by way of international agreement, see:

- 1970 Hague Convention of the Suppression of Unlawful Seizure of Aircraft;
- 1971 Montreal Convention for the Suppression of Unlawful Acts against the Safety of Civil Aviation;
- 1973 Convention on the Suppression and Punishment of the Crime of Apartheid;
- 1980 Convention on the Prevention and Punishment against Internationally Protected Persons including Diplomatic Agents;
- 1984 Convention against Torture and Other Cruel Inhuman or Degrading Treatment or Punishment, see also *R v Bow Street Metropolitan Stipendiary Magistrate Ex parte Pinochet Ugarte No.3* [2000] 1 A. C. 147; and *Filartiga v Pena-Irala* (see above p.37);
- 1988 Convention against Illicit Traffic in Narcotic Drugs (1989); and
- 2001 Convention on Cybercrime.

Such agreements require contracting parties to either apprehend and charge alleged offenders or, alternatively, extradite alleged offenders. Such obligations are applicable to contracting parties only and the "political offence exception plea" may be invoked to deny extradition.

THE PASSIVE PERSONALITY PRINCIPLE

This refers to jurisdiction being exercised on the basis of the victim's nationality. It was not recognised in the Harvard Draft Convention *(above)* but it has received limited recognition, see art.5(1)(c) of 1984 UN Torture Convention which provides:

"Each state shall take such measures as may be necessary to establish its jurisdiction over the offences referred to in art.4 in the following cases;

... (c) when the victim is a national of that state if that state considers it appropriate."

See also the *Cutting Incident* 1887, the *Achille Lauro Incident* 1985 and the case of the *US v Yunis* (No 2) 681 F. Supp. 896 (1998).

There is no hierarchy of bases of jurisdiction. Factors such as the custody of the alleged offender determine which state will ultimately exercise jurisdiction.

THE INTERNATIONAL CRIMINAL COURT (ICC)

Offences over which the ICC has jurisdiction are the most serious crimes of international concern, e.g. genocide, crimes against humanity, war crimes and the crime of aggression.

DEFINITION CHECKPOINT
The Complementarity Principle
The ICC supplements domestic legal systems and will prosecute only if domestic courts are unwilling or unable to do so. This is known as the complementarity principle. For the ICC to have jurisdiction:
" ... one or more of the parties involved is a State Party; the accused is a national of a State Party; the crime is committed on the territory of a State Party; or a State not party to the Statute may decide to accept the ICC's jurisdiction over a specific crime that has been committed within its territory, or by its national", art.1 of Statute of ICC.

Before the ICC has jurisdiction one of the following must occur: the ICC Prosecutor must have referred a matter to the Court; the Security Council has referred a matter to the Prosecutor for the ICC; or the Prosecutor for the ICC undertakes an investigation under his own initiative, in accordance with art.13 of the Statute of the ICC.

Extradition

DEFINITION CHECKPOINT
Extradition
The means whereby an alleged offender, found in the territory of a state other than the State seeking to exercise jurisdiction, is handed over by the former to the latter.

Extradition is regulated by treaty, however where there is no treaty, there is no duty to extradite.

Illegal apprehension

There is no consistent practice regarding instances of illegal apprehension, however, illegal apprehension in itself does not preclude exercise of jurisdiction, see the cases of the *US v Toscanino* 500 F. (2d) 207 (1974) (US Court of Appeals) and compare this with the case of the *US v Alvarez-Machain* (1992) 31 I.L.M. 902 and *Sosa v Alvarez-Machain et al* (2004) 542 US, decided June 29, 2004—together with *US v Alvarez-Machain (above))*.

IMMUNITY FROM JURISDICTION

Sovereign Immunity

DEFINITION CHECKPOINT
Par in parem non habat imperium One cannot exercise authority over an equal.

Historically, a Sovereign and his or her state were regarded as synonymous, and the ruler of a foreign state continues to enjoy complete immunity for acts done in a private capacity, see *Mighell v Sultan of Johore* [1894]. However, today states are engaged in an increasing number of commercial activities which prompted a modification of the absolute immunity principle of state enterprises.

The contemporary situation is that immunity will be granted for *jure imperii* (government acts) but not for acts *jure gestionis* (trading and commercial acts).

KEY CASE
For one example of absolute immunity see the *Parlement Belge case* (1879) 4 Pd 129. In the *Parlement Belge case* (1880) 5 Pd 197 the Court of Appeal reversed the decision of the lower court and upheld the vessel, the Parlement Belge, as the property of the King of Belgium, enjoyed immunity, and immunity recognised under customary international law.

The moves towards a more restrictive immunity began in the 1950s and 1960s with the US State Department "Tate Letter" of 1962, and the case law of the central European courts. The former provided, " ... the immunity of the Sovereign is recognised with regard to sovereign or public acts—*jus imperii*—of a state, but not with respect to private acts *(jus gestionis)*", 6 Whiteman, 569–571.

The European judicial decisions similarly restricted grant of absolute immunity to government acts, but only those government acts which could be categorised as *jure imperii*. This restriction to sovereign immunity was regarded as necessary because otherwise state enterprises, when engaged in commercial activities, enjoyed a more privileged position than non-state enterprises.

The UK and Commonwealth countries did not follow suit until the 1970s, but decisions in the *Philippine Admiral* [1977] A.C. 373, J.C.; the *Trendtex Trading Corporation v Central Bank of Nigeria* (see above, p.34) and *I Congreso del Partido* [1981] 3 W.L.R. 329, H.L. paved the way for the **State Immunity Act of 1978**.

The 1972 European Convention on State Immunity identifies the circumstances in which sovereign immunity is applicable, see also the Draft UN Convention on Jurisdictional Immunities of States and Their Property 2004, opened for signature in 2005. This sets out a general principle of immunity, art.5, subject to certain exceptions, art.10–17.

Restrictive immunity is now the norm and is generally accepted by states.

Diplomatic Immunity

Diplomatic immunity represents an exception to the exercise of territorial jurisdiction. Diplomatic relations are one of the earliest expressions of international law. It has long been accepted that a foreign state's representative is immune from a host state's domestic law.

Customary international law for the most part is reflected in the Vienna Convention on Diplomatic Relations 1961—the 1961 Vienna Convention—although some of the articles do represent progressive development. This Convention sets out immunities of foreign diplomatic missions and foreign diplomatic personnel in a receiving host state. Diplomatic relations are founded on the mutual consent of states. The purposes of diplomatic immunity, and the privileges that flow from diplomatic relations, is a functional one, that is, the rules are designed to promote and facilitate the functioning of diplomatic representation. The host state must give its assent to *(agrément)* the diplomatic agent (Head of Mission). Refusal of *agrément* does not require reasons. The host state may declare the Head of Mission, or any member of the diplomatic staff, a *persona non grata*—the person is not acceptable. Persons so designated must be recalled or his position terminated by the sending state. The functions of a diplomatic mission are spelt out in art.3 of the 1961 Vienna Convention as:

"... (a) representing the sending State in the receiving State;
   (b) protecting in the receiving State the interests of the

sending State and of its nationals within the limits
permitted by international law;

(c) negotiating with the government of the receiving State;

(d) ascertaining by all lawful means conditions and
developments in the receiving Sate, and reporting thereon
to the government of the sending State;

(e) promoting friendly relations between the sending State and
the receiving State, and developing their economic, cultural
and scientific relations."

Premises of a mission—are inviolable and must not be entered by agents of
the receiving state without permission. The receiving state must afford protection to mission premises. Article 22 of the 1961 Vienna Convention provides immunity from search, requisition, attachment or execution to mission
premises and their internal effects. This inviolability extends to the private
residence of a diplomatic agent, his or her papers and his or her correspondence. This was reflected in the *Case Concerning U.S. Diplomatic and
Consular Staff in Tehran (Provisional Measures)* (1979) I.C.J. Rep. 7; and in the
merits judgment I.C.J. (1980) Rep. 3 in which the Court stated:

"The inaction of the Iranian Government by itself constituted
clear and serious violations of Iran's obligations to the United
States under the provisions of Article 22, para. 2 and Articles 24,
25, 26, 27 and 29 of the 1961 Vienna Convention on Diplomatic
Relations ... "

Individuals of a mission—Diplomats enjoy absolute immunity from criminal
jurisdiction of the receiving state and immunity from civil and administrative
jurisdiction, except in three specific instances:

(a) a real action relating to private immovable property situated in the
territory of the receiving State, unless he holds it on behalf of the
sending State for the purposes of the mission;

(b) an action relating to succession in which the diplomatic agent is
involved as executor, administrator, heir or legatee as a private person
and not on behalf of the sending State and;

(c) an action relating to any professional or commercial activity exercised
by the diplomatic agent in the receiving State outside his official
functions, art.37 (1) *(above)*.

A diplomatic agent (under the 1961 Vienna Convention either the Head of the
Mission or a member of the diplomatic staff of the Mission) is not liable to

arrest or detention and not obliged to give evidence as a witness, art.31(2). This immunity is extended to the family of the diplomatic agent if they are non-nationals of the host state, art.37. If a national, then immunity is limited to performance of official functions only, art.38.

Note, immunity refers to the jurisdictional immunity and not immunity from liability. The right to immunity may be waived by the sending state, however it must be expressed, art.32(1)).

Diplomatic staff members are now differentiated, and categories of staff are defined in the 1961 Vienna Convention. This differentiation of staff was an innovation in the 1961 Vienna Convention and led to different degrees of immunity being enjoyed. The degree of immunity corresponds to the designated category of staff. The relevant article is art.37, which provides that:

"The members of the family of a diplomatic agent forming part of his household shall, if they are not nationals of the receiving State, enjoy the privileges and immunities specified in arts 29 to 36", (i.e. all the immunities enjoyed by the diplomatic agent).

Non-national administrative and technical staff members are granted, together with members of their families forming part of their respective households, absolute immunity from criminal jurisdiction, but only from civil and administrative jurisdiction with regard to official duties. Non-national service staff members enjoy immunity only with regard to official acts. Private servants of members of the mission shall, if they are not nationals of or permanently settled in the receiving state, be exempt from dues and taxes on the emoluments they receive by reason of their employment. In other respects, they may enjoy privileges and immunities only to the extent admitted by the receiving state. However, the receiving state must exercise its jurisdiction over those persons in such a manner as not to interfere unduly with the performance of the functions of the mission. See the 1973 Convention on the Prevention and Punishment of Crimes against Internationally Protected Persons, including Diplomatic Agents.

If a diplomat is recalled or declared *persona non grata* he/she does not lose immunity immediately. However on expiry of a "period of grace" the individual may be sued for private acts undertaken during his or her period in office. Immunity remains for official acts. Diplomatic agents and mission premises are also immune from most taxes levied in the host state.

The diplomatic bag must be marked as such and may not be opened or detained, art.27(3). However, it is now established that there exists a right of challenge. If the bag is challenged the sending state has two possible courses of action:

(1) the bag may be returned to the sending state unopened;

(2) consent is given to the bag being opened and inspected.

See the attempts by the ILC to put forward principles on this subject in the 1989 Draft articles on the Status of the Diplomatic Courier and the Diplomatic Bag not Accompanied by the Diplomatic Courier. Draft art.28 acknowledges the inviolability of the diplomatic bag but does allow a receiving state or a transit state to request the opening of a bag if there are suspicions to warrant such a request. However, the Draft articles have not as yet been adopted.

The law on immunities for consular staff and those employed in special missions are set out in 1963 Vienna Convention on Consular Relations and the 1969 Convention on Special Missions.

Heads of State

KEY CASE

PINOCHET IN THE UK

For cases concerning heads of state and their position regarding immunity see *R. v Bow Street Metropolitan Stipendiary Magistrate Ex p. Pinochet Ugarte* (No 2) [2001] 1 A.C. 119, *R. v Bow Street Stipendiary Magistrate Ex p. Pinochet Ugarte* (No.3) [2000] (*above*); *R. v Bartle and the Commissioner of Police for the Metropolis Ex p. Pinochet,* [1991] 2 All E.R. 97, *R. v Evans and the Commissioner of the Police for the Metropolis Ex p. Pinochet* 24 March 1999, House of Lords and *the Arrest Warrant case* (see above, p.106). The outcome of the *Pinochet* case was that a former Head of State would only enjoy immunity for those acts carried out within his official function as Head of State. However what is an official act and what is a personal act remains unresolved. It was also held in *Pinochet* that neither an individual nor a state could claim immunity for acts prohibited by an international Convention to which the state claiming the immunity is a contracting party. The relevant date in Pinochet was 1986, the year Chile ratified the Convention Against Torture and Other Cruel, Inhuman or Degrading Treatment or Punishment.

The *Case Concerning the Arrest Warrant (Congo v Belgium)* (2002) (see above, p.106) endorsed the immunity of a DRC national who at the time of his offence was the Minister for Foreign Affairs.

Note also the Alien Tort Claims Act 1789 (ACTA) which provides that District Courts have jurisdiction in any civil actions raised, "by an alien for a tort only, committed in violation of the Law of Nations or a treaty of the United States." See also the 1991 Torture Victim Prevention Act.

In March 2009 the ICC issued an arrest warrant for Omar Hasan Ahmad Al Bashir, the President of Sudan, on charges of crimes against humanity and war crimes. This was the first time the ICC had indicted a sitting Head of State. This has proved to be a controversial move, dividing opinion throughout the international community on its merits.

Revision Checklist

You should now know and understand:

- What is understood by state jurisdiction;

- The principal bases of jurisdiction;

- Where these principles were spelt out;

- The subjective and objective territorial principles, and their differences;

- The principle on which the *Arrest Warrant Case* was an attempt to found jurisdiction;

- The crime regarded as the true international crime;

- Examples of crimes susceptible to universal jurisdiction;

- The meaning of the passive personality principle;

- Whether illegal apprehension of an alleged offender precludes the exercise of jurisdiction;

- The necessity of restricting the absolute immunity of state enterprises;

- The significance of the distinction between *jure imperii* and *jure gestionis*;

- The purpose of diplomatic immunity;

- The extent of the diplomatic mission's immunity;

- The scope of a diplomat's immunity from criminal jurisdiction;

- The scope of a diplomat's immunity from civil and administrative jurisdiction;

- How the Vienna Convention on Diplomatic Relations distinguishes the staff of a diplomatic mission;

- The consequences of the distinction for the various categories of staff;

- The Convention which regulates the immunities for consular staff and;

- The US Act employed to seek civil redress from US corporations for alleged breaches of human rights.

QUESTION AND ANSWER

The Question

Discuss the following:

(a) Would a "diplomatic agent" who negligently injures a pedestrian while on a motoring holiday in a receiving state be entitled to claim immunity in respect of civil or criminal proceedings under the Vienna Convention on Diplomatic Relations 1961, if both the sending and state in which he is accredited are parties to the Convention?

(b) Would a filing clerk or a domestic servant employed in the embassy be entitled to plead immunity in the same circumstances?

(c) What would the position be if the "offending" person was a spouse or a private employee of any of the above persons?

(d) Might the nationality or the place of permanent residence of the person claiming immunity in any of the above cases be relevant?

Advice and the Answer

The position of each individual in the respective scenarios should be examined within the context of the relevant provisions of the 1961 Vienna Convention on Diplomatic Relations. Mention should be made of the way in which the Vienna Convention by distinguishing various categories of staff marks a departure from the established pre 1961 position.

Human Rights

11

INTRODUCTION

International human rights law deals with the protection of individuals and groups from violations of their internationally guaranteed rights and the promotion of these rights. This is distinct from humanitarian law, which is the human rights law component of the law of armed conflict.

RECOGNITION AFFORDED TO INDIVIDUALS

Pre–1945 there is little evidence of protection afforded to individuals under international law other than in minority treaties, trusteeship and non self-governing systems. Slavery has been contrary to customary international law since 1815.

Note the Slavery Convention 1926 and supplementary Convention on the Abolition of Slavery, the Slave Trade and Institutions and Practices Similar to Slavery 1956. However only post–1945 has there been any attempt to afford universal protection of human rights.

A stated purpose of the UN is:

> "to achieve international co-operation ... in promoting and encouraging respect for human rights and for fundamental free-doms for all without distinction as to race, sex, language or religion".

The UN Charter arts 55 and 56 call upon the United Nations and Member States to achieve, inter alia:

> "universal respect for, and observance of, human rights and fundamental freedoms for all without distinction as to race, sex, language and religion."

However, note the UN Charter does not impose a hard obligation on Member States to achieve anything within a set time frame. Articles 55 and 56 are thus examples of soft law. For a further explanation of soft law see Ch.2 on Sources.

The Universal Declaration of Human Rights (UDHR) 1948 was adopted as a General Assembly Resolution (and thus not binding) on December 10, 1948. The UDHR sets out a wide range of political, civil, economic, social and cultural rights designed as a, "common standard of achievement for all peoples of all nations," Mrs Eleanor Roosevelt, Chair of the UN Commission on Human Rights.

UDHR

There are 30 articles in the UDHR relating to the rights and freedoms which are regarded as being every person's birthright and which are to be enjoyed without distinction of any kind such as race, colour, sex, language, religion, political or other opinion, national or social origin, property, birth or other status. These rights are only to be curtailed by:

> "such limitations as are determined by law solely for the pur-
> poses of securing due recognition and respect for the rights and
> freedoms of others and of meeting the just requirements of
> morality, public order and the general welfare in a democratic
> society", art.29(2).

Articles 1 and 2 of UDHR are seen as fundamental principles underlying all human rights. Articles 3–21 consist of civil and political rights and arts 22–27 refer to economic, social and cultural rights. The last three articles provide a framework of solidarity safeguarding the universal enjoyment of all human rights.

Article 1	Right to freedom and equality in dignity and rights
Article 2	Freedom from discrimination
Article 3	Right to liberty, and security of persons
Article 4	Freedom from slavery and servitude
Article 5	Freedom from torture or degrading treatment
Article 6	Right to recognition as a person before the law
Article 7	Right to equal consideration before the law
Article 8	Right to remedy through a competent tribunal
Article 9	Freedom from arbitrary arrest or exile
Article 10	Right to a fair trial or public hearing
Article 11	Right to be considered innocent until proven guilty

Article 12   Freedom from interference with privacy, including home, family and correspondence

Article 13   Right to freedom of movement and residence in one's own country and to leave and return at will

Article 14   Right to asylum

Article 15   Right to a nationality and freedom to change it

Article 16   Right to marriage and protection of family

Article 17   Right to own property

Article 18   Freedom of belief and religion

Article 19   Freedom of opinion and information

Article 20   Right to peaceful assembly and association

Article 21   Right to participate in government and in free elections and to equal access to public service.

Article 22   Right to social security

Article 23   Right to work and fair pay for work

Article 24   Right to rest and leisure

Article 25   Right to adequate standard of living for health and well-being

Article 26   Right to education

Article 27   Right to participate in the cultural life of the community

Article 28   Right to social order assuring human rights

Article 29   Responsibility to the community for the free and full development of every individual

Article 30   Freedom from state or other interference in any of the above rights.

Note, 1948 also saw the adoption of the Convention on the Prevention and Punishment of the Crime of Genocide 1948.

The rights and freedoms contained in UDHR are further spelt out in the two UN Covenants—the International Covenant on Civil and Political Rights 1966—ICCPR, frequently referred to as First Generation Rights—which entered into force in March 1976 and the International Covenant on Economic, Social and Cultural Rights 1966—ICESCR, Second Generation Rights—which entered into force in January 1976. Together these three instruments are often referred to as the International Bill of Rights.

Figure 3: International Bill of Rights

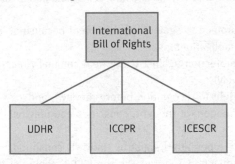

The ICCPR

Article 2(1) of ICCPR calls upon contracting parties:

> "to respect and to ensure to all individuals within its territory and subject to its jurisdiction the rights recognised in the present Covenant".

The obligation on contracting parties is to realise the rights immediately upon ratification.

The rights protected by the ICCPR are reflected within arts 3–21 of the UDHR. The ICCPR explicitly prohibits torture, cruel, inhuman or degrading treatment or punishment, slavery, servitude and forced or compulsory labour.

Restrictions may be imposed on the exercise of a right but such a restriction must be provided by law and be necessary in the interests of national security, public order, public health or morals, or for the protection of the rights and freedoms of others.

Derogation is allowed in times of a public emergency, "which threatens the life of the nation and the existence of which is officially proclaimed," but parties to the ICCPR may only take such:

> "measures derogating from their obligations ... to the extent strictly required by the exigencies of the situation, provided that such measures are not inconsistent with their obligations under international law and do not involve discrimination solely on the ground of race, colour, sex, language, religion or social origin", art.4(1).

Derogation in respect of the ICCPR is prohibited by art.4(2). These articles are:

- Article 6 (the inherent right to life);
- Article 7 (prohibition of torture, cruel, inhuman or degrading treatment);

- Article 8 (prohibition of slavery and being held in servitude, paragraphs 1 and 2);
- Article 11 (protection against imprisonment because of inability to fulfil contractual obligations);
- Article 15 (protection against being held criminally responsible for acts retrospectively);
- Article 16 (right to recognition before the law); and
- Article 18 (freedom of thought, conscious and religion).

Derogations, where permitted, must be narrowly construed.

The Second Optional Protocol to the ICCPR, aiming at the Abolition of the Death Penalty 1989, calls upon contracting parties to take all necessary measures to abolish the death penalty within their jurisdiction. The Second Protocol entered into force in 1991.

The ICESCR
Article 2(1) of ICESCR requires a contracting party:

> "to take steps ... to the maximum of its available resources, with a view to achieving progressively the full realisation of the rights recognised in the present Covenant."

The obligation on contracting parties is to take what steps it can but there is no specific time frame for compliance. The rights protected by the ICESCR are reflected within arts 22–27 of the UDHR.

Over and above the rights contained in the UDHR, both Covenants recognise the right of all peoples to self-determination and the right to, "freely dispose of their natural wealth and resources", Common art.1.

Other international Conventions specifically for the protection of the individual include:

- International Convention on the Elimination of All Forms of Racial Discrimination 1966;
- International Convention on the Elimination of All Forms of Discrimination Against Women 1979;
- International Convention against Torture and other Cruel, Inhuman or Degrading Treatment Punishment 1985;
- International Convention on the Rights of the Child 1989;
- International Convention on the Protection of the Rights of all Migrant Workers and Members of their Families 1990;
- International Convention on the Rights of Persons with Disabilities 2006.

COMPLIANCE MECHANISMS

Reporting Systems

Reporting systems involve the submission by contracting parties of a periodic report to a committee. Both Covenants include reporting systems. In the case of the ICCPR—the Human Rights Committee; and the ICESCR—the Committee on Economic Social and Cultural Rights (CESCR) (see below).

ICCPR: contracting parties are required to report within one year of becoming a contracting party and thereafter at intervals determined by the Human Rights Committee. The Human Rights Committee consists of 18 individuals sitting in their individual capacity. The Human Rights Committee's role is to report and make, "such general comments as it may consider appropriate to the States parties."

ICESCR: contracting parties are required to submit reports, "in stages, in accordance with a programme to be established by the Economic and Social Council within one year of the entry into force of the present Covenant after consultation with the States Parties and the specialised agencies concerned," art.17. The provision "stages" was amended in 1988 so that a state's report is now required to include all Covenant rights. The Economic Social and Cultural Rights Committee gives a concluding observation in respect of a State's performance; forwards a yearly report to Economic and Social Council (ECOSOC) and issues General Comments on a wide variety of topics, such as General Comment No. 4—the right to adequate housing; General Comment No.5—regarding persons with disabilities and General Comment No. 12—the right to adequate food.

The Reporting systems, as set out above, are common to both Covenants. The aim of the reporting system was spelt out in CESCR General Comment 1:

> " ... that it would be incorrect to assume that reporting is essentially a procedural matter designed solely to satisfy each State Party's formal obligation to report to the appropriate international monitoring body. On the contrary, in accordance with the letter and spirit of the Covenant the process of preparation and submission of reports by States can, and indeed should, serve to achieve a variety of objectives", para 1.

Inter-State Complaint

Under the ICCPR, a state may initiate a "complaint" against another state provided both states have accepted art.41 and local remedies have been exhausted. The alleged right violated must be a right protected by ICCPR. This "complaint" seeks conciliation and "friendly" settlement.

Note, art.41 has never been employed.

Other Conventions with inter-state complaint procedures are the Torture Convention (optional), art.21 and the Convention on the Elimination of All Forms of Racial Discrimination (compulsory), art.11.

Individual communication

The Human Rights Committee may by way of the First Optional Protocol to the ICCPR (entered into force March 1976) receive communications from individuals alleging a breach of an ICCPR right by a contracting party. The communication must identify the alleged victim, must relate to a Covenant right, must not be under consideration in any other international body and all domestic remedies must have been exhausted. The role of the Committee is to examine applications and then forward the Committee's views to the state party concerned and the individual as to whether there has been a breach. The Committee is not a judicial body, applications are considered in private with no oral hearing and the Committee's views published in annexes attached to the annual report.

In 2008, the Economic, Social and Cultural Committee adopted an Optional Protocol to the ICESCR. This provides that communications may be submitted by, or on behalf of, individuals or groups of individuals under the jurisdiction of a state party claiming there has been a breach of a right protected by the ICESCR. This Optional Protocol is now open for signature.

Other Conventions have recognised the individual communication procedures, e.g. art.14 (optional) of the Convention on Racial Discrimination, see *Yilmaz-Dogan v Netherlands* (1988) C.E.R.D. Report, G.A.O.R., 43rd Session, Supp. 18, 59. This was the first case to invoke art.14 successfully. The questions raised were whether the Netherlands had failed to meet its obligations under art.5(e)(i) to guarantee equality before the law in respect of the right to work and protection against employment; and whether arts 4 and 6 of the Racial Convention imposed on contracting parties an obligation to bring criminal proceedings in cases of alleged racial discrimination and to provide for an appeal mechanism in cases of such discrimination. CERD formed the view that Mrs Yilmaz-Dogan's dismissal was a result of a failure to take into account all the circumstances surrounding her case and that of her right to work under art.5(e)(i) had not been protected. CERD maintained it was:

> " ... of the opinion that the information as submitted by the parties sustains the claim that the petitioner was not afforded protection in respect of her right to work. The Committee suggests that the State party take this into account and recommends that it ascertain whether Mrs Yilmaz-Dogan is now gainfully employed and, if not, that it use its good offices to secure

alternative employment for her and/or to provide her with such other relief as may be considered equitable", para.10.

There is also an Optional Protocol to the Convention on the Elimination of Discrimination Against Women, art.2, which provides for individual petition against a consenting contracting party, which entered into force in 2000. See *Ms. B-J v Germany* (Communication Number 1/2003) (Decision adopted July 14, 2004). In this decision the communication was declared inadmissible. However, in the case of *Ms AT v Hungary* (Communication Number 2/2003) (Decision adopted January 26, 2005) the Committee held that Hungary had failed to take appropriate steps to prevent and protect women from domestic violence. Hungary had not exercised the appropriate due diligence, albeit that the perpetrator was a private individual.

An Optional Protocol to the Torture Convention entered into force in 2006. Under the Optional Protocol States are to set up, designate or maintain, at the domestic level, one or more bodies for the prevention of torture and other cruel, inhuman or degrading treatment or punishment, art.3.

The following two cases are examples of instances where an individual has been able to pursue redress for violation of their human rights:

- In *Lovelace* Human Rights Committee (1981) 2 Selected Decisions 28, it was held there was a violation of art.27 of the ICCPR by a provision of Canadian legislation. Under the Indian Act (Canada), a woman was prevented from returning to her Indian Reserve following the dissolution of her marriage to a non-Indian;
- See also *Mauritian Women* 1981 Report of the Human Rights Committee 166, in which Mauritian legislation whereby Mauritian women with a foreign national spouse (Mauritian men with a foreign spouse were not so disadvantaged) were at risk of deportation was held to be contrary to the ICCPR. However Mauritian men with a foreign spouse were not so disadvantaged.

Individuals may derive protection from a number of different sources. For instance: the General Assembly by virtue of art.13(b) of the UN Charter, which provides the General Assembly shall:

" ... initiate studies and make recommendations for the purpose of promoting international co-operation in the economic, social, cultural educational and health fields and assisting in the realisation of human rights and fundamental freedoms for all without distinction as to race, sex, language or religion"

INTERNATIONAL LAW

Compliance Mechanisms by Instrument

Figure 4: International Covenant on Civil and Political Rights 1966

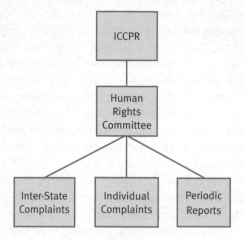

Figure 5: International Covenant on Economic, Social and Cultural Rights 1966

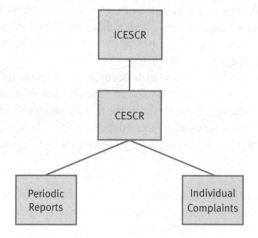

Figure 6: International Convention on the Elimination of All Forms of Racial Discrimination 1966

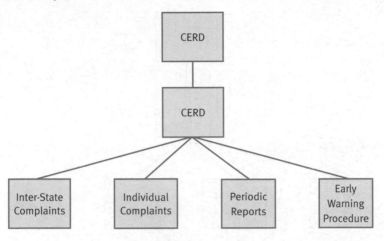

Figure 7: International Convention on the Elimination of All Forms of Discrimination Against Women 1979

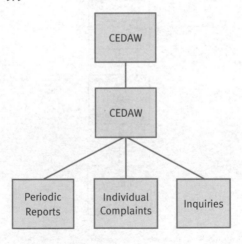

Figure 8: International Convention against Torture and other Cruel, Inhuman or Degrading Treatment Punishment 1985

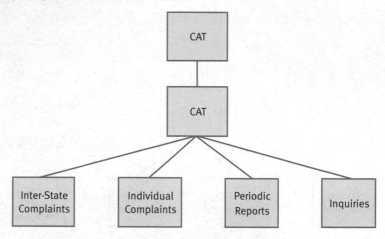

Figure 9: International Convention on the Rights of the Child 1989

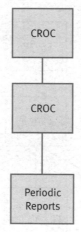

Figure 10: International Convention on the Protection of the Rights of all Migrant Workers and Members of their Families 1990

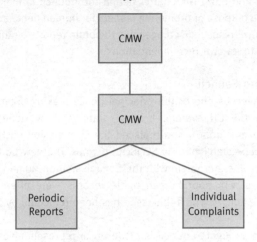

Figure 11: International Convention on the Rights of Persons with Disabilities 2006

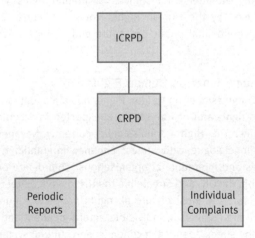

ECOSOC

Articles 62(2) and 62(4) UN Charter permit the Council to make recommendations for the purpose of promoting respect for human rights and for making arrangements, with specialised agencies to obtain reports on the steps taken to give effect to its own recommendations.

Human Rights Council

This is envisaged as one of the principal policy making organs for Human Rights within the UN system. It was established by General Assembly Resolution 60/251 (2006), and replaced the Commission on Human Rights which had been established by ECOSOC in 1946. The new body was established to overcome a problem with the Commission on Human Rights where Member States with poor human rights records were often represented. However, the extent to which this issue has been remedied by the new body is contested.

The Human Rights Council is made up of representatives from 47 UN Member States who are elected by secret vote by a majority of Member States in the General Assembly. It has a very broad mandate, primarily to strengthen the promotion and protection of human rights globally. It does this by drawing attention to instances of human rights violations. The mechanisms used by the Human Rights Council comprise special public procedures, a confidential public procedure and a novel universal periodic review.

UN High Commissioner on Human Rights

The UN High Commissioner on Human Rights has a mandate to promote and protect human rights and ensure they are respected in accordance with the relevant treaties. The High Commissioner—currently Navanethem Pillay—must engage in dialogue with states; enhance international co-operation between states and international organisations; co-ordinate promotion and protection within the UN; and streamline the UN to work better to reach these goals. To this end she must ensure all rights political, cultural, economic, social and civil are "universal, indivisible, interdependent and interrelated" regardless of the states "political, economic, and cultural system". She must also recognise the importance of the right to development and as such promote and protect the realisation of that right by encouraging all states to also recognise this right.

ECOSOC Resolution 42/1235 was adopted in 1967 to examine information relevant to gross violations of human rights and, "to study situations, which reveal a consistent pattern of violations of human rights". Resolution 42/1235 (XLII) has provided the basis for the Human Rights Commission to initiate:

1) investigations within States of alleged violations of human rights; and
2) the establishment of Working Groups, Special Rapporteurs and Expert Bodies to consider human rights situations, for example the Working Group on Enforced and Involuntary Disappearances (1980) and the Working Group on Arbitrary Detention (1991).

In addition, a number of Rapporteurs have been given the responsibility of mandates regarding specific countries e.g. Haiti and Rwanda. Other Rapporteurs have been given responsibility for particular behaviour and rights, such as religious intolerance, sale of children, education, and the right to adequate housing. Country specific mandates are reviewed annually and thematic mandates every three years. Although charged with this responsibility the Special Rapporteurs and Experts depend upon the co-operation of States and governments and of course they only report to the Human Rights Commission and do not have any means of enforcing their views.

ECOSOC Resolution 48/1503—now considerably revised since introduced initially in 1970—provides for a working group to examine, in private, individual petitions, and to consider those which reveal a consistent pattern of gross and reliably attested violations of human rights. If it is decided in the affirmative the matter is referred to the Working Group on Situations, which then decides whether to refer the matter to the Sub-Commission on the Promotion and Protection of Human Rights. The 1503 procedure is confidential and before communications can be received all domestic remedies are required to have been exhausted.

The Human Rights Committee
The Human Rights Committee is the body which monitors the ICCPR (see above, p.119).

The Human Rights Committee is a body established pursuant to the ICCPR, art.28. It consists of 18 experts nominated and elected by contracting parties. The Committee meets three times a year for four week sessions. Members sit in their personal, independent capacity and are elected for a four-year term, after which they are eligible for re-nomination. As in all UN organs an equitable, geographical distribution is sought.

Regarding inter-state complaints the Human Rights Committee makes its good offices available to the states concerned, see art.41 ICCPR. The emphasis is on conciliation and there is, for instance, no mechanism for reference to a judicial body. Although in existence for almost thirty years this procedure has not been employed.

Initially an individual communication has to be assessed regarding admissibility and, if admissible, the merits of the case are considered by the Human Rights Committee. The Human Rights Committee may propose a particular remedy although the norm is to leave the remedy to the state concerned. The offending state is given 90 days within which to advise the Human Rights Committee of the remedy adopted. The Human Rights Committee's views are not binding and they publish an annual report in which defaulting states are identified.

The Human Rights Committee has developed a corpus of norms regarding the interpretation of the Covenant, e.g. the requirement that there be a victim, i.e. *Mauritian Women* (see above, p.123) where it was stated the risk of being affected adversely has to be more than just a theoretical possibility.

The Human Rights Committee also produces General Comments. These are designed to provide clarification in the interpretation of articles contained in the Covenant, e.g. the right to life as guaranteed by art.6 of the ICCPR.

The ESCR Committee

The ESCR Committee is also made up of 18 members elected by ECOSOC from a list of nominees submitted by state parties. Members are elected for four years and elections are staggered, taking place every two years. Members may be re-elected. Again, representation on the ESCR Committee is based on equitable geographical distribution.

CONVENTIONAL MECHANISMS

Enforcement mechanisms are provided under a variety of different Human Rights Conventions. The most common forms of machinery include:

- Reports submitted by states and examined by relevant Committees, normally established under the specific international human rights instrument;
- Individual petitions and/or inter-state Complaints, e.g. art.14 of the Convention on the Elimination of All Forms of Racial Discrimination allows for the acceptance of individual complaints (see above, p.122);
- Specialised Agencies of the United Nations, e.g. International Labour Organisation (ILO);
- The Optional Protocol to CEDAW, entered into force 2000;
- The Optional Protocol to the Convention on the Rights of the Child Concerning the Sale of Children, Child Prostitution and Child Pornography, entered into force 2002;
- The Optional Protocol to the Convention on the Rights of the Child on the Involvement of Children and Armed Conflict, entered into force 2002;

- The Optional Protocol to the Torture Convention, entered into force 2006; and
- *Cases:* The work of these bodies and others has led to the development of a substantial body of jurisprudence in this area, e.g. *Weinberger case*, Report of the Human Rights Committee, G.A.O.R., 36th Session, Supp. 40, 114; *Vuolanne v Finland* (1989) H.R.C. Rep. G.A.O.R., 44th Session, Supp. 40, 249; and *NG v Canada* Human Rights Committee (1994) 1–2 I.H.R.R. 161.

See also for example: Resolution 40/144 (1985) Regarding the Human Rights of Individuals who are not Nationals of the Country in which they Live (United Nations); *Barcelona Traction* case (see above, p.9) obligations *erga omnes*.

PRINCIPAL STANDARD SETTING INSTRUMENTS AND INSTITUTIONS AT A REGIONAL LEVEL

- European Convention on Protection of Human Rights and Fundamental Freedoms 1950, inter-state complaint—art.33; individual petition—art.34;
- The European Court of Human Rights;
- European Social Charter 1961;
- European Convention for the Prevention of Torture and Inhuman and Degrading Treatment or Punishment 1987;
- American Convention on Human Rights 1970;
- African Charter on Human and Peoples' Rights 1981 (Banjul Charter); and
- Arab Charter on Human Rights 1994, revised 2004.

Revision Checklist

You should now know and understand:

- The efforts to protect human rights prior to 1945;
- The relevant provisions in the UN Charter which seek the promotion of human rights;
- The intentions of the Universal Declaration of Human Rights;
- The nature of the rights spelt out in the Universal Declaration;
- The two Covenants responsible for setting out these rights and freedoms in greater detail;

- The human rights identified as non-derogable;

- The requirements for contracting parties under the Second Optional Protocol to the ICCPR;

- The obligations of States under the ICESCR;

- The compliance mechanisms of the ICCPR and the ICESCR;

- The significance of the First Optional Protocols;

- The Human Rights Committee; The other Conventions which have provision for individual communication;

- The role of the Human Rights Council;

- Some regional Conventions which seek to afford protection to individuals;

- Some other UN Human Rights Conventions.

QUESTION AND ANSWER

The Question

How effective is the United Nations in affording protection to human rights?

In your answer highlight the principal weaknesses and suggest how such perceived deficiencies could best be overcome.

Advice and the Answer

Initially the way in which the UN attempts to protect human rights should be discussed. The UN's commitment as reflected in the UN Charter may be identified. The Declaration on Human Rights and the international human rights instruments should be highlighted but focus primarily should be made on the mechanisms for monitoring compliance by contracting parties. One approach would be to look at the reporting mechanism and the relative strengths and weaknesses of that against the right of individual petition. Note the question is focusing on the weaknesses.

Alan and Bobby are members of a linguistic minority (Toys) living in the southern part of Funland. They were arrested on suspicion of involvement in terrorist activities aimed at achieving independence for the Toys. Following their apprehension Alan and Bobby were questioned for six days during which time they were deprived of sleep, food and were threatened with torture unless they divulged what they knew to the Funland authorities. Bobby remained silent and was physically tortured and subsequently died from the injuries sustained. Alan did provide relevant information, which led to the police finding a cache of weapons. Alan was then sent to a camp in a remote northern part of the country and was detained there for two years with other suspected terrorists. He was released in March as part of an amnesty precipitated by the announcement from the Toy leadership that they were renouncing violence.

Funland is a party to the International Covenant on Civil and Political Rights and its First Optional Protocol.

Alan is now seeking legal advice as to whether he can initiate a claim against the Funland government for a violation of his human rights. Alan has also been contacted by Bobby's sister who wishes to take action against the Funland government in respect of her brother's death. Advise Alan and Bobby's sister.

Advice and the Answer

The significance of Funland being a party to the ICCPR and the Protocol should be highlighted. The next issue is the locus standi of Alan. Focus should then be on what it is Alan is claiming has been violated, i.e. which Article of the Covenant. As for Bobby's sister the issue is whether she can be considered a victim. In this respect reference should be made to the *Mauritian Women's* case. What constitutes torture may be considered and the issue of whether there is an alternative avenue of redress, for at least Alan, may be raised.

Judicial Settlement of International Disputes

12

INTRODUCTION

According to art.2(3) of the UN Charter states are obliged to, "settle their international disputes by peaceful means in such a manner that international peace and security, and justice, are not endangered." The peaceful settlement of disputes is also recognised as a rule of customary international law.

For there to be settlement required there must be a dispute.

> **DEFINITION CHECKPOINT**
> *Dispute*
> An international dispute is defined as "a disagreement on a point of law or fact, a conflict of legal views of interests between two persons." (I.e. that is international persons), see *Mavrommatis Palestine Concessions case* (1924) P.C.I.J. Ser. A No 2 at 11–12.

See also Resolution 25/2625 (1970) Declaration on Principles of International Law Concerning Friendly Relations and Co-operation among States (United Nations), and Resolution 37/10 (1982) Manila Declaration on Peaceful Settlement of International Disputes (United Nations).

MODES OF SETTLEMENT

The UN Charter, art.33(1) provides that:

> "The parties to any dispute, continuance of which is likely to endanger the maintenance of international peace and security, shall first of all, seek a solution by negotiation, enquiry, mediation, conciliation, arbitration, judicial settlement, resort to regional agencies or arrangements, or other peaceful means of their own choice."

Article 33(2) provides that,

"The Security Council shall, when it deems necessary, call upon the parties to settle their dispute by such means."

NEGOTIATION

There is an obligation on states to enter:

" ... into negotiations with a view to arriving at an agreement ... they are under an obligation so to conduct themselves that the negotiations are meaningful, which will not be the case when either of them insists upon its own position without con-templating any modification of it", *North Sea Continental Shelf case* (see above, p.7), at 47.

The ICJ in this case thus set out the scope and extent of the obligation.
   Normally only parties to the dispute are involved in negotiation, how-ever a third party may bring disputing states to the negotiating table through good offices.

ENQUIRY

Commission of Enquiry—the function of such a Commission is to establish the facts. The Commission may hear witnesses and visit relevant places involving the dispute. A Commission of Enquiry may be established by an international organisation.

MEDIATION

Is a process, which as a norm will most likely involve a third party, who may suggest ways of possibly reconciling the respective position and claims of the parties involved.

CONCILIATION

Is usually when a Commission is appointed to examine the claims and it may make suggestions for resolution of the dispute. Such suggestions are not binding.

ARBITRATION

Is defined as a procedure for the settlement of disputes between states by a binding award on the basis of law, and as a result of an undertaking, voluntarily accepted, the International Law Commission 1953.

Modern arbitration history may be traced from the:

* 1794 Jay Treaty between the UK and the US;
* 1871 Treaty of Washington also between the UK and the US;

See also, e.g. the *Alabama Claims Arbitration* Moore, 1 Int. Arb. 495 (1872) where the disputing parties, Britain and the US, each nominated a member to the Arbitration Tribunal. Three independent states also nominated a member. These states were Brazil, Italy and Switzerland.

* 1899 Convention on the Pacific Settlement of International Disputes, which set up the Permanent Court of Arbitration established in 1900. In 1907 the Convention on the Pacific Settlement of International Disputes revised the 1899 Convention but retained the Court. The Permanent Court of Arbitration began functioning in 1902, but is neither a Court nor is it permanent. Rather, it is a panel of some 300 individuals, any one of whom may be called upon to constitute a Tribunal for the settlement of a particular dispute.

The Conventions adopted model rules on arbitration procedure which may be referred to in arbitration agreements.

Other procedural rules include Resolution 13/1262 (1958) International Law Commission Model Rules on Arbitral Procedure (United Nations).

Arbitration is regarded favourably as a mechanism for the settlement of disputes because it allows parties to the dispute a greater say in, e.g. membership of the tribunal, the law to be applied and the effect of the award. Such details are set out in what is known as the *Compromis*.

JUDICIAL SETTLEMENT

The Permanent Court of International Justice (PCIJ) functioned as of 1922 until being formerly dissolved in 1946 following the dissolution of the League of Nations. It should be noted that the PCIJ was not an integral body of the League of Nations, although there was close association between the two organisations.

The PCIJ's successor was the International Court of Justice (ICJ). The ICJ is the principal judicial organ of the UN under art.92 of the UN Charter. The ICJ is composed of fifteen judges, of which no two judges may be nationals of the same state. Judges are elected by the Security Council and General Assembly. Article 2 of ICJ Statute states that persons eligible for appointment are those:

"of high moral character, who possess the qualifications required in their respective countries for appointment to the highest judicial offices, or are jurisconsults of recognised competence in international law".

These judges are appointed for a nine-year term and may be re-elected. Five Judges are elected every three years and the judges elect a President and Vice-President from their number for a term of three years. The President and Vice-President may be re-elected.

The ICJ has its own rules of court and possesses the jurisdiction to hear contentious cases and deliver advisory opinions. The ICJ may also be called upon to exercise incidental jurisdiction, hear preliminary objections, and applications to intervene and indicate interim measures. The law applied by the ICJ is found in art.38(1) ICJ Statute. See Ch.3 Sources above.

Contentious cases

> **DEFINITION CHECKPOINT**
> *Ratione personae*
> Only states may be party to a contentious case before the ICJ, for consideration of locus standi see case *Concerning the Application of the Convention on the Prevention and Punishment of the Crime of Genocide (Bosnia and Herzegovina v Yugoslavia Serbia and Montenegro) (1993) (Indication of Provisional Measures in 1993)* I.C.J. Rep. 325.

> **DEFINITION CHECKPOINT**
> *Ipso Facto*
> That very fact or act.
> All UN members are ipso facto parties to the ICJ Statute. A non-UN member may become a party to the ICJ Statute on conditions prescribed by the UN General Assembly following a Security Council recommendation.

A state neither party to the UN nor the ICJ Statute may make a special declaration, which may be either "particular" or "general". A state must give its consent to appearing before the ICJ, see case *Concerning East Timor*

(Portugal v Australia) (1995) I.C.J. Rep 90, endorsing the, "well established principle of international law embodied in the ICJ's Statute, namely, that the ICJ can only exercise jurisdiction over a state with its consent." The principle had been expounded in the *Monetary Gold Removed from Rome in 1943* (1954) I.C.J. Rep. 32.

Acceptance of the ICJ's jurisdiction may be by way of art.36(1) whereby the ICJ has jurisdiction over cases:

> "which States in a dispute may agree to refer to it and all matters specially provided for in the Charter of the United Nations or in treaties and conventions in force."

Acceptance of the ICJ's jurisdiction under art.36(1) is frequently by way of special agreement (*compromis*) between the parties to a dispute, as in, e.g. the *Asylum* case (1950) I.C.J. Rep. 266; and the *Minquiers and Echros* case (1953) I.C.J. Rep. 47.

Many bipartite and multipartite treaties make express provision for reference to the ICJ as a dispute resolution mechanism.

Acceptance of the ICJ's jurisdiction need not be in a prescribed format, *Corfu Channel (Preliminary Objections)* case (1948) I.C.J. Rep. 15. In this case a letter addressed by the Albanian government to the ICJ was held to constitute a voluntary acceptance of the Court's jurisdiction.

DEFINITION CHECKPOINT
Forum prorogatum
This term refers to instances in which a state unilaterally initiates proceedings before the ICJ and the other state by its conduct can be inferred to have consented.

Instances of *forum prorogatum* seldom arise, see *Mavromatis Merits* case (see above, p.134) where the ICJ held that its jurisdiction arose in respect of a particular issue, "in consequence of an agreement between the parties resulting from the written proceedings ... " See also *Anglo-Iranian Oil Co* case (1952) I.C.J. Rep. 93.

Note also the rules of the ICJ art.38(5) providing:

> " ... where the applicant State proposes to found the jurisdiction of the Court upon a consent thereto yet to be given or manifested against which such application is made, the application shall be transmitted to that state. It shall not however be entered in the General List, nor any action be taken in the proceedings, unless

and until the State against which such application is made consents to the Court's jurisdiction for the purpose of the case."

See application of art.38(5) in the case *Concerning Certain Questions of Mutual Assistance in Criminal Matters (Djibouti v France)* [2008] I.C.J. Rep, paras 39–95.

Optional Clause

Acceptance may also be by way of art.36(2)—the "optional" clause. A declaration under art.36(2) is not compulsory but once such a declaration has been made reference to the ICJ is required. Relatively few states have made such a declaration. Cases, which have been lodged under art.36(2), include the *Temple* case (1962) I.C.J. Rep. 6 and the *Arrest Warrant case* (see above, p.114). An undertaking made under art.36(2) applies only in respect of other states accepting the same obligation, i.e. the condition of reciprocity jurisdiction is only to the extent the declarations of the parties overlap. States may also insert a reservation (condition) to an art.36(2) declaration, art.36(3). The effect of reciprocity is to allow, "the State which has made the wider acceptance of the jurisdiction of the ICJ to rely upon the reservations to the acceptance laid down by the other party. There the effect of reciprocity ends." *Interhandel* case I.C.J. Rep. 1959 6 and *Nicaragua* case (1984) I.C.J. Rep. 551. See also the *Norwegian Loans* case (1957) I.C.J. Rep. 9—in which the reservation contained in the applicant state's declaration was relied upon by the defendant state to deny the ICJ jurisdiction.

Reservations made under art.36(3) may be with respect to time— *ratione temporis*—or subject matter—*ratione materiae*.

Declarations under art.36(2) are frequently made for a stated time period—e.g. five years as in the case of the UK—and may be terminated unilaterally on notice. A temporal declaration cannot be terminated retroactively to exclude the ICJ's jurisdiction. Declarations must be valid at the time proceedings are initiated but modification or expiry subsequent to the ICJ being validly seised of the case will not negate the ICJ's jurisdiction.

For consideration of what is referred to as the multilateral treaty reservation see the *Nicaragua case (above)*. The multilateral treaty reservation operates so as to exclude disputes, "arising under a multilateral treaty" and demands that, "all parties to the treaty affected by the decision be parties to the case before the Court." Such a reservation was contained in the 1946 US Declaration accepting the ICJ's jurisdiction under art.36(2). The US in the *Nicaragua* case (*above*) attempted to deny the ICJ jurisdiction by invoking that reservation. The ICJ however did not accept the US argument.

The decisions of the ICJ are given by a majority and dissenting judgements and separate opinions are published. A dissenting judgement is one which disagrees with the decision reached. A separate opinion is one which agrees with the decision, but sets out separate legal reasoning. The effect of the ICJ's judgments has no binding force except between the parties to the case. The decision of the ICJ is final. However, a request for an interpretation of the judgment may be made on request by either of the parties to the dispute. A request may be made for a revision of the decision, art.61, if a new fact emerges that was previously unknown to the requesting state or the ICJ.

Incidental jurisdiction

Preliminary objections: Refers to an objection to the ICJ exercising jurisdiction to the case. This occurs when one state (normally the respondent state) raises an objection as a preliminary matter. Proceedings on the merits are halted until the ICJ gives a decision on the preliminary objections. Such objections must be lodged within three months of the applicant state submitting the memorial.

An application to intervene, art.62: May be requested by a state not a party to the dispute before the ICJ, but the state believes it has a legal interest in the outcome of the case. See *Tunisia v Libyan Arab Jamahiriya (request by Malta)* (1981) I.C.J. Rep. 3 and the *Land, Island and Maritime Frontier Dispute (request by Nicaragua)* (1992) I.C.J. Rep. 92. There is an onus on the requesting state to demonstrate a legal interest.

Interim measures, art.41: the ICJ:

> "has the power to indicate, if it considers that circumstances so require, any provisional measures which ought to be taken to preserve the respective rights of either party."

The ICJ will exercise such jurisdiction if it deems it necessary so as to "protect rights which are the subject of the dispute", see *Aegean Sea Continental Shelf* case (1976) I.C.J. Rep. 3. Requests for interim measures are considered promptly and, if the ICJ decides in the affirmative, interim orders may be made requesting the contesting parties refrain from action that would intensify the dispute or render resolution more difficult. Interim measures are only indicated and only issued if the ICJ feels it has jurisdiction over the substantive matter of the dispute. See the *La Grand* case (2001) 40 I.L.M. 1069, for further discussion of the character of interim measures and the conclusion that, "the contention that provisional measures indicated under art.41 might not be binding would be contrary to the object and purpose of that article."

For a discussion on the ICJ's possible competence to review measures of the Security Council, see the dissenting opinion of Judge Weeramantry in the case *Concerning Questions of Interpretation and Application of the Montreal Convention Arising out of the Ariel Incident at Lockerbie (Provisional Measures)* (1992) I.C.J. Rep. 3.

Advisory opinions of the ICJ are not legally binding but have contributed to the development of international law, see art.65, and the *Legal Consequences of the Construction of a Wall in the Occupied Palestinian Territory* 2004.

The ICJ will decline to give an opinion if to do so would in effect be making a decision in a dispute, see *Eastern Carelia case* (1923) P.C.I.J. Rep. Ser. B No. 5.

Note, a further range of mechanisms may also be used to settle a dispute, for example Regional Organisations have provided machinery for dispute settlement—i.e. the OAS; the Arab League; and the OSCE.

Other judicial/quasi-judicial bodies:

- International Tribunal for the Law of the Sea, see Ch.8 above
- European Court of Justice
- European Court of Human Rights
- I.C.T.Y.—International Tribunal for the Prosecution of Persons Responsible for Serious Violations of Humanitarian Law Committed in the Territory of the Former Yugoslavia
- I.C.T.R.—International Tribunal for the Prosecution of Persons Responsible for Genocide and Other Serious Violations of International Humanitarian Law Committed in the Territory of Rwanda and Rwandan Citizens Responsible for Genocide and Other such Violations Committed in the Territory of Neighbouring States, between 1 January 1994 and 31 December 1994
- International Criminal Court, see Ch.9 above
- Sierra Leone Special Court
- The World Trade Organisation

Revision Checklist

You should now know and understand:

- **What is understood by the term "international dispute";**
- **The methods of dispute settlement identified in art.33 of the UN Charter;**

- The extent of the obligation to negotiate;

- The definition of arbitration;

- Why the term "Permanent Court of Arbitration" is somewhat anomalous;

- The distinction between arbitration and judicial settlement;

- How the ICJ may be seised of jurisdiction;

- *Forum prorogatum;*

- The shortcomings of art.36(2);

- The effect of the ICJ's decision in a contentious case;

- The incidental jurisdiction of the ICJ;

- Advisory Opinions and their contribution to the development of international law;

- Who has locus standi to seek an Advisory Opinion;

- The nature of other judicial bodies on the international scene.

QUESTION AND ANSWER

The Question

As a Government legal adviser, you have been requested to prepare a memorandum highlighting the advantages and disadvantages of judicial settlement of international disputes.

In your memorandum consider the relative merits of judicial settlement over other peaceful methods of international dispute settlement.

Advice and the Answer

The answer requires identification of dispute settlement means other than judicial, e.g. negotiation, mediation and arbitration etc. Reference should be made to art.33 of the UN Charter. Judicial settlement should be considered and the particular characteristics of this mode of dispute settlement discussed. The relative strengths and weaknesses regarding the other identified mechanisms should be examined, e.g. binding decision, impartial body, cost, length of proceedings etc.

Use of Force

13

INTRODUCTION

Jus ad bellum is the right to wage war, a right initially enjoyed by sovereigns. The right to wage war is no longer regarded as a legitimate instrument of national policy and is prohibited under contemporary international law.

Efforts to control and regulate the use of force stem from 1928 and the General Treaty for the Renunciation of War—the Kellogg-Briand Pact. Prior to 1928 the use of force was not prohibited. Contracting parties to the Kellogg-Briand Pact were required to seek a peaceful resolution to disputes arising between them.

The Kellogg-Briand Pact is now superseded by the UN Charter. The UN Charter seeks to regulate the use of force and identifies when its use may be lawful. The general rule is that there exists a prohibition on the use of force, save in certain circumstances. UN Member States are required by art.2(3), "to settle their international disputes by peaceful means in such a manner that international peace and security, and justice are not endangered".

Article 2(4) requires that all Member States:

> "Shall refrain in their international relations from the threat or use of force against the territorial integrity or political independence of any State, or in any manner inconsistent with the purposes of the United Nations."

Article 2(4) is now regarded as customary international law and the requirement to abstain from the use of force is acknowledged as a *jus cogens* norm. Article 2(4) prohibits not only the use of force but also the threat of such and extends to include, e.g. reprisals. See the *case Concerning Military and Paramilitary Activities In and Against Nicaragua (Merits)* (see above, p.9 at 100).

Note, Article 2(4) makes explicit reference to force against the territorial integrity or political independence of any state, as well as the use of force in any manner inconsistent with the purposes of the UN. The purposes of the UN are set out in art.1 of the UN Charter with the primary purpose being the maintenance of international peace and security, and peaceful resolution of disputes.

Prohibition on the use of force is elaborated upon in Resolution 25/2625 (1970) Declaration on Principles of International Law Concerning Friendly Relations and Co-Operation Among States in Accordance with the Charter of the United Nations (United Nations).

For a definition of aggression see:

- the Resolution 29/3314 (1974) Definition of Aggression (United Nations);
- the 1996 Draft Code of Crimes against the Peace and Security of Mankind, art.12; and
- the Resolution 42/22 (1987) Declaration on the Enhancement of the Effectiveness of the Principle of Refraining from the Threat or Use of Force in International Relations (United Nations).

Aggression is regarded as a crime against the peace for which there is responsibility under international law. However, note that although the ICC has competence to exercise jurisdiction over crimes of aggression, a definition of what constitutes aggression has yet to be agreed. Only then will the ICC's jurisdictional competence be established.

Article 2(4) only prohibits the use of force between states, i.e. inter–state but not within a state, i.e. intra-state. See Resolution 20/2131 (1965) Declaration on the Inadmissibility of Intervention in the Domestic Affairs of States and the Protection of their Independence and Sovereignty (United Nations) and also Resolution 25/2625 (1970) (above).

REPRISALS (COUNTER MEASURES)

Reprisals are illegal acts under international law normally resorted to by a state and adopted in retaliation in response to having been on the receiving end of an unlawful act. See Resolution 25/2625 (1970) (above), expressly prohibiting reprisals, "States have a duty to refrain from acts of reprisals involving the use of force."

Reprisals should be compared with retorsions.

RETORSIONS

Retorsions are a lawful means of expressing disapproval at another state's conduct. The state's conduct is not illegal but may for example be unfriendly, discourteous, or unfair and inequitable. Whether a retorsion is justified is something which should be decided on a case by case basis.

RIGHT OF A STATE TO USE FORCE IN SELF-DEFENCE

Article 51 of the UN Charter permits a state to exercise its inherent right of individual or collective self-defence, that is, if an armed attack occurs against a member of the UN. The right of self-defence subsists **until** the Security Council has taken measures necessary to maintain international peace and security.

KEY CASE

Case Concerning Military and Paramilitary Activities in and against Nicaragua (Merits) (*above*), which, in paras 103–104, determines what constitutes an armed attack:

"There now appears to be general agreement on the nature of the acts which can be treated as constituting armed attacks. In particular, it may be considered to be agreed that an armed attack must be understood as including not merely action by regular armed forces across an international border, but also "the sending by or on behalf of a State armed bands, groups, irregulars or mercenaries, which carry out armed force against another State of such gravity as to amount to" (inter alia) an actual armed attack conducted by regular forces, "or its substantial involvement therein ... " The Court sees no reason to deny, that in customary international law, the prohibition of armed attacks may apply to the sending by a State of armed bands to the territory of another State, if such an operation, because of its scale and effects, would have been classified as an armed attack rather then a mere frontier incident had it been carried out by regular armed forces. But the Court does not believe that the concept of "armed attack" includes not only acts by armed bands where such acts occur on a significant scale but also assistance to rebels in the provision of weapons or logistical or other support. Such assistance may be regarded as a threat or use of force, or amount to intervention in the internal or external affairs of other States."

Also in this case the ICJ found the right of self-defence under art.51 and the content of customary international law to be the same, however, in customary international law there is no obligation to report to the Security Council.

The criteria to be fulfilled for the use of force in self-defence, is as established in the *Caroline Incident* 29 B.F.S.P. 1137–1138: 30 B.F.S.P. 195–196. The need must be:

- instant;
- overwhelming;
- immediate; and
- there is no viable alternative action possible.

The foregoing criteria were set out in the correspondence to the British Government from the US Secretary of State Webster. The *Caroline Incident* concerned a ship, the Caroline, which supplied rebel insurrectionaries in Canada. The Caroline, which operated out of US territory, was destroyed by British Officers and two US nationals were killed. A UK subject, McLeod, was arrested on charges of murder and arson and Secretary of State's Webster's letter was part of the correspondence which ensued between the US and British authorities. In addition to the criteria set out, Secretary of State Webster emphasised the need for the act of self-defence to be neither unreasonable nor excessive—i.e. proportionate.

The fact that force used in self-defence should be no more than that necessary to counter the attack—i.e. proportionate—has been reiterated since, see case *Concerning Military and Paramilitary Activities in and against Nicaragua (Merits)* (see above, p.9).

In the *Oil Platforms (Merits)* case (2003) *(Iran v United States)* I.C.J. Rep. the ICJ concluded that actions carried out by US forces against Iranian oil installations could not be justified:

> " ... as being measures necessary to protect the essential security interests of the US, since those actions constituted recourse to armed force not qualifying, under international law on the question, as acts of self-defence, and thus did not fall within the category of measures contemplated, upon its correct inter-pretation, by that provision of the Treaty."

See also Security Council Resolution 1368, adopted September 12, 2001, in which the Security Council endorsed, "the inherent right of individual or collective self-defence in accordance with the Charter." Endorsed by Security Council Resolution 1373, adopted September 28, 2001.

For a state to afford assistance to another state pursuant to its right of collective self-defence, the state under attack must request assistance, see case *Concerning Military and Paramilitary Activities in and against Nicaragua (Merits)* (see above, p.9):

> "The exercise of the right of collective self-defence presupposes that an armed attack has occurred: and it is evident that it is the victim State, being the most directly aware of the fact, which is likely to draw general attention to its plight. It is also evident that if the victim State wishes another State to come to its help in the exercise of the right of collective self-defence, it will normally make an express request to that effect. Thus in the present instance, the Court is entitled to take account, in judging the asserted justification of the exercise of collective self-defence by the United States, of the actual conduct of El Salvador, Honduras and Costa Rica at the relevant time, as indicative of a belief by the States in question of a request by the victim State to the United States for help in the exercise of collective self-defence."

USE OF FORCE TO PROTECT NATIONALS ABROAD

States may employ force to protect nationals who are seen as being at risk abroad. The basis on which this is done is by invoking a legal fiction whereby a threat to nationals is interpreted as tantamount to a threat to the state of nationality. Examples of intervention to protect nationals include the Israeli raid on Entebbe Airport, Uganda in 1976 and American interventions in Grenada 1983 and Panama 1989. Intervention in such instances is premised on the host state's failure to protect non-nationals to at least a minimum international standard. The use of force in such instances should be used restrictively as entering another state's territory without consent amounts to a violation of territorial integrity and sovereignty, see art.2(7) UN Charter and see below.

The right to use force in anticipation of an armed attack remains a controversial issue, as art.51 of the UN Charter refers to armed attack only. A right of anticipatory self-defence is argued as existing under customary international law. On that basis if state B threatens state A with the use of force state A can argue that a legitimate response is the use of force.

USE OF FORCE BY STATES THROUGH THE UN

The Security Council can authorise military sanctions against a state following an affirmative decision that a particular situation constitutes a threat, e.g. a breach of the peace or act of aggression. Such a determination is made under art.39 of the UN Charter and lies exclusively within the discretion of the Security Council. See the dissenting opinion of Judge Weeramantry in the case *Concerning Questions of Interpretation and Application of the Montreal Convention Arising out of the Ariel Incident at Lockerbie (Provisional Measures)* (see above, p.141):

> "Chapter VI entrusts it [Security Council] with powers and responsibilities in regard to settlement of disputes, and Chapter VII gives it very special powers when it determines the existence of any threat to the peace, breach of the peace or act of aggression. Such determination is a matter entirely within its discretion."

Note, the Resolution 5/377 (1950) Uniting for Peace (United Nations), whereby if the Security Council is unable to fulfil its responsibilities for the maintenance of international peace and security the matter may, if ostensibly an art.39 matter, be considered by the General Assembly.

The Security Council may, under art.42, authorise the use of armed force as may be necessary to maintain or restore international peace and security. Article 42 will only be invoked if the Security Council considers that art.41 measures have been, or would be, inadequate.

Article 41 measures are those not involving the use of force. These may include:

> "complete or partial interruption of economic relations and of rail, sea, air, postal, telegraphic, radio, and other means of communication, and the severance of diplomatic relations."

Article 42, is supplemented by art.43, whereby Member States:

> " ... undertake to make available to the Security Council, on its call and in accordance with a special agreement or agreements, armed forces, assistance and facilities, including rights of passage, necessary for the purpose of maintaining international peace and security."

However, the agreements envisaged in art.43 have not materialised, largely because of the "Cold War" and the use of the veto by permanent members of the Security Council.

HUMANITARIAN INTERVENTION

Humanitarian intervention is when force is used to afford protection to the nationals of a state other than those of the intervening state(s). Most frequently the individuals being protected will be nationals of the territorial state. The right of humanitarian intervention is not clearly established in international law:

> " ... in fact, the best case that can be made in support of humanitarian intervention is it cannot be said to be unambiguously illegal ... In essence, therefore, the case against making humanitarian intervention an exception to the principle of non-intervention is that its doubtful benefits would be heavily outweighed by its costs in terms of respect for international law", UK Foreign Office Policy Document Number 148, (1986).

However, note the "*UK Guidelines on Humanitarian Intervention*" (2000) 71 *B.Y.I.L.* 646. These guidelines identified six principles on which to build a framework to guide intervention by the international community. Most importantly it was acknowledged that for intervention there must be convincing evidence of extreme humanitarian distress on a large scale requiring urgent relief. It must be objectively clear that there is no practicable alternative to the use of force to save lives. Any use of force should be proportionate to achieving the humanitarian purpose and must be carried out in accordance with international law. The scale of potential or actual human suffering justifies the dangers of military action and this action must be likely to achieve its objectives. Any use of force should be collective, in other words no individual country can assert that it is using military action on behalf of the international community.

In 2001, the International Commission on Intervention and State Sovereignty (ICISS), an independent international body established by the Canadian Government, elaborated the doctrine of "Responsibility To Protect" (R2P). The ICISS identified three elements to the doctrine: prevention, reaction to situations of compelling human need, and rebuilding.

In 2004, a UN High-Level Panel on Threats, Challenges and Change endorsed in its report, "the emerging norm that there is a collective international responsibility to protect". The doctrine was also endorsed by the General Assembly at the 2005 World Summit, reaffirmed by the Security

Council in 2006—Resolutions 1674 and 1706—and by the Secretary-General in 2009—The Report to the General Assembly 63rd Session. Although a number of states support the doctrine, including the UK and Canada, its position in contemporary international law remains unsettled.

FORCE AUTHORISED BY A UN ORGAN

A state may be authorised by the Security Council to use force in situations when such force would otherwise be unlawful, see Security Council Resolution 221/1966. Question concerning the situation in Southern Rhodesia (United Nations).

NON-INTERVENTION

Article 2(7) of the UN Charter provides the UN shall not intervene, "in matters which are essentially within the domestic jurisdiction of any State or shall require the members to submit such matters to settlement under the present Charter."

Note however the principle of non-intervention does not apply with respect to enforcement measures taken pursuant to Ch.7.

COLLECTIVE REGIONAL ARRANGEMENTS

UN Charter art.52(1) recognises that regional arrangements or agencies may deal with the maintenance of international peace and security provided such activities and agencies are compatible with the purposes and principles of the UN. Article 52(2) emphasises pacific settlement of local disputes through regional arrangements or agencies. Article 54 requires the Security Council be kept fully informed.

Collective self-defence organisations, such as NATO, have art.51 UN Charter as their legal basis. Article 5 of the NATO Treaty provides that an armed attack on one member shall be treated as an attack on all members.

DEFINITION CHECKPOINT
Jus in Bello
The *jus in bello* relates to the legal regime regulating the conduct of hostilities.
Historically it was divided into two branches:

1. The Law of The Hague: regulating methods and means of warfare—i.e. weapons—see primarily Hague Conventions 1899 and 1907; and
2. The Law of Geneva: which dealing with the protection afforded to individuals, e.g. prisoners of war and civilians, the four 1949 Geneva Conventions and the two 1977 additional Protocols to the Geneva Conventions.

Today it is acknowledged the two bodies of law are closely inter-related and form one single complex system known as international humanitarian law, see *Advisory Opinion on the Legality of the Threat or Use of Nuclear Weapons* (1996) I.C.J. Rep. 226. Regarding nuclear weapons there is a recognised obligation on states to negotiate in good faith for international nuclear disarmament, see the above case *Advisory Opinion on the Legality of the Threat or Use of Nuclear Weapons* (see above).

Note, the Geneva Conventions were initially applicable only to international armed conflict, however they were extended to wars of self-determination in Protocol 1 1977 and non-international—i.e. internal—armed conflicts in Protocol 2.

. . . .

UN PEACEKEEPING

See Boutros Boutros Ghali, "An Agenda for Peace Preventive Diplomacy, Peacemaking and Peacekeeping", 1992 which identified important interconnected UN security functions. One proposal was for the creation, under art.43 of the UN Charter, of permanent peace enforcement units. Article 43 provides that UN Member States are to conclude agreements with the Security Council with the necessary forces to carry out military enforcement measures. As stated above, however, these agreements were never concluded and states supply military forces voluntarily. These peacekeeping forces, which must remain at all times impartial, have been deployed extensively throughout the world on a wide variety of functions, e.g. ceasefire supervision; patrol of buffer zones; and supervising withdrawal of occupying forces.

For the constitutionality of peacekeeping forces see ICJ *Advisory Opinion Certain Expenses of the UN* (see above, p.25), in which it acknowledged the residual role of the General Assembly with the regard to the maintenance of international peace and security.

There is an ongoing review of UN peace and security activities, see Brahimi Report 2000. See also General Assembly Resolution 60/180 (2005) The Peacebuilding Commission (United Nations), establishing a

Peacebuilding Commission as an inter-governmental advisory body. The main purposes of the commission are set out as being:

"... (a) To bring together all relevant actors to marshal resources and to advise on and propose integrated strategies for post conflict peacebuilding and recovery;

(b) To focus attention on the reconstruction and institution-building efforts necessary for recovery from conflict and to support the development of integrated strategies in order to lay the foundation for sustainable development;

(c) To provide recommendations and information to improve the co-ordination of all relevant actors within and outside the United Nations, to develop best practices, to help to ensure predictable financing for early recovery activities and to extent the period of attention given by the international community to post conflict recovery."

Revision Checklist

You should now know and understand:

- The *jus cogens* status of the prohibition of the use of force contained in art.2(4) of the UN Charter;

- The scope of art.2(4);

- The scope of a state's right to use force in self-defence;

- The importance of the *Caroline* case;

- The doctrines of humanitarian intervention and responsibility to protect;

- The circumstances in which the Security Council can authorise military sanctions;

- The criteria that must be satisfied before collective self-defence can be exercised;

- The areas of law which make up the *jus in bello*;

- The effect of the non-fulfillment of art.43 of the UN Charter;

- The legal effect of the ICJ's opinion in the *Certain Expenses of the UN*.

QUESTION AND ANSWER

The Question

The prohibition of force under contemporary international law is absolute.

Critically discuss.

Advice and the Answer

The answer should start by acknowledging that it is not absolute and that international law seeks to control the use of force. The current position can be traced from the Kellogg-Briand Pact as prior to this the use of force was considered legitimate state action. The UN Charter reflects the efforts to control the use of force and implores states to refrain from resorting to force in their relations with each other. The UN Charter acknowledges the right of self-defence as subsisting under customary international law and endorses, in art.51, the right to self-defence. The answer could also discuss anticipatory self-defence and whether or not this is allowed, as well as the various views on the nature and scope of art.2(4). The answer should also consider humanitarian intervention and its legitimacy in international law.

Handy Hints and Useful Websites

14

HANDY HINTS

Concerning the exam it is important to read the question and answer the question asked. Take time to read the examination paper and identify the questions, which you are going to attempt. Answering an examination question successfully does not necessarily mean writing down all you know on a particular subject. You have to approach the question as required, i.e. discuss, analyse, evaluate and you have to be discriminating in the way you present your information. It is advisable to make an "answer plan", i.e. a skeleton answer. This provides a good checklist as you write your answer and a reference point once you have completed your answer.

It is important to allocate sufficient time to each answer.

Exam papers will normally be made up of a mix of questions demanding either an essay type answer or a step by step legal analysis of a hypothetical case scenario. In the former remember what you are being asked to do, e.g. discuss, analyse, evaluate, remember to avoid generalisation and substantiate your statements. In a case scenario read the "case" and step by step identify the legal issues involved. In a case scenario you will be acting, very often, as legal adviser and you should present your answer in such a manner endorsed by the relevant contemporary case law.

EXAMINATION REVISION CHECKLIST

A good way to revise is to revisit the revision checklist found at the end of each chapter and test yourself against the points highlighted. Also go over again the sample exam questions at the end of each chapter, but bear in mind these, as set out in this Nutshell Guide, are designed to deal only with the matter dealt with in the individual chapters. Questions set in actual examinations will of course not be so clear cut in defining the issues involved and will most likely raise a number of issues relating to different facets of international law. Below you will find an example of such a question.

QUESTION AND ANSWER

The Question

The Solaris Embassy is besieged by members of the illegal Prot Fighters who are active in the State of Paxis. After some days a number of the group break rank and gain entry to the Solaris Embassy, where they take the Solarisian Ambassador hostage. Solaris orders Paxis not to intervene, however Paxis cuts all communication lines with the Embassy. Consequently the Ambassador is denied any contact with his home state of Solaris.

Paxisian security forces set up roadblocks throughout the country and begin an extensive search for the fighters. At one road block the Solarisian Embassy car is stopped and the body of an individual who had evidently been tortured is discovered in the boot. The driver of the car, a nephew of the Solarisian Ambassador, is arrested.

Solaris seeks to initiate an action in the International Court of Justice against Paxis for its failure to observe the relevant principles of international law.

Paxis has made an unqualified declaration accepting the jurisdiction of the International Court of Justice whereas Solaris, not a member of the United Nations, has accepted the jurisdiction of the International Court of Justice in all matters "except those within its domestic jurisdiction as determined by the courts of Solaris".

Solaris's Foreign Minister seeks your advice as to the legal issues involved. Prepare a legal memorandum addressing the relevant legal issues arising.

Advice and the Answer

Legal issues involved—main issue is whether the ICJ has jurisdiction necessary to look at the nature of the declaration made by the respective parties and the effect of Solaris's reservation. The relevant case law includes the *Norwegian Loans case*, the *Interhandel case*, and the *Nicaragua Merits case*. Secondary legal issues are those of diplomatic law, the scope of inviolability of mission premises and the immunity of diplomatic personnel and their relatives. The answer should be written in the form of a memorandum.

USEFUL WEBSITES

The electronic resources for international law are extensive. Some of the principal ones are identified below and should not be regarded as exhaustive.

http://www.un.org—The United Nations

http://www.bayefsky.com—The UN Human Rights Treaties

http://www.ohchr.org—UN Office of the High Commissioner for Human Rights

http://www.unhcr.org—UNHCR

http://www.unicef.org—UNICEF

http://www.icty.org/—ICTY

http://www.ictr.org/—ICTR

http://www.icj-cij.org/—ICJ

http://www.ilo.org/ilolex/english/iloquerymtn1.htm—ILO Tripartite Declaration of Principles concerning Multi-national Enterprise's and Social Policy

http://www.echr.coe.int—European Court of Human Rights

http://www.icrc.org—International Committee of the Red Cross

http://www.itlos.org—Tribunal for the Law of the sea

http://www.amnesty.org—Amnesty International

http://www.hrw.org/—Human Rights Watch

http://www.asil.org—American Society of International Law, particularly useful INSIGHTS (essays relating to current international issues)

http://www.eisil.org/—useful for all elements of international law

http://library.ukc.ac.uk/library/lawlinks/default.htm—University of Kent, useful as a starting point for research

http://news.findlaw.com/legalnews/international—useful for up to date international issues

http://www.law.cornell.edu/topics/international.html—useful for research

http://www.globalcompact.org—UN Global Compact

http://www.oecd.org/—OECD

Latin terms

Ad hoc—	For this purpose.
Animus—	Intention.
De facto—	Existing as a matter of fact.
De jure—	Existing as a matter of law.
Ex aequo et bono—	The ICJ has the power, if the parties to a contentious case agree, to take a decision, not on the basis of the sources limited to art.38(1) of the ICJ Statute.
Forum prorogatum—	Term, which describes the case where, by agreement of the parties, the case is submitted to a judge other than the judge ordinarily competent in the matter.
Hostis humani generis—	An enemy of the human race.
Inter se—	This doctrine is still acceptable to the extent that some aspects of inter se relationships are governed by the Conventions of the Commonwealth rather than international law.
Ipso facto—	That very fact or act.
Jure imperii—	Acts performed in a governmental or public capacity.
Jure gestionis—	Acts performed in a commercial or private capacity.
Jus ad bellum—	Refers to the right to make war.
Jus cogens—	See arts 53 and 64 of 1969 Vienna Convention on the Law of Treaties. Otherwise known as peremptory norms of international law. The term is founded in customary international law and is so fundamental it binds all states. No states can derogate from this and it can only be modified by a subsequent norm of international law with the same character.

Jus in bello—	Relates to the laws and customs of war.
Locus standi—	Right of standing before the court.
Non liquet—	Inability to decide due to lack of a legal source.
Obiter dicta—	Something said by a judge, which is not essential to the decision of the case but is nonetheless relevant.
Obligations erga omnes—	Obligations owed to the international legal community as a whole and obligations, which every state has an interest in having respected.
Opinio juris sive necessitatis—	Is an essential element of custom. It requires that a state practice have legal obligations.
Pacta sunt servanda—	See art.26 1969 Vienna Convention on the Law of Treaties. Agreements are binding upon parties to it and must be performed by them in good faith.
Pacta tertiis nec nocent nec prosunt—	Third parties receive neither rights nor duties from contracts.
Par in parem non habat imperium—	One cannot exercise authority over an equal.
Persona non grata—	The term refers to ambassadors or other diplomatic agents who are personally unacceptable to the receiving government.
Ratione personae—	Relates to persons standing before the court.
Ratione temporis—	This term relates to time.
Ratione materiae—	The term refers to the nature of a dispute or subject matter of that dispute.
Rebus sic stantibus—	Through a fundamental change of circumstance, international law recognizes that treaties may cease to be binding upon the parties.
Stare decisis—	The decisions of the ICJ have no binding force except between the parties and in respect of that particular case.
Terra nullius—	Unclaimed land. The term is used in relation to discovery and is a method of acquiring territorial sovereignty.
Uta possedtis juris—	Seen as a general principle of international law. The term is derived from the Spanish (South American), where the boundaries of former colonies were deemed to constitute the boundaries of newly independent successor states.

Glossary of abbreviations

AU	African Union; previously known as the Organisation of African Unity (OAU)
AJIL	American Journal of International Law
ASIL	American Society of International Law
AYBIL	Australian Yearbook of International Law
BYIL	British Yearbook of International Law
CEDAW	Convention on the Elimination of all Forms of Discrimination against Women
CSR	Corporate Social Responsibility
ECHR	European Convention of Human Rights
ECtHR	European Court of Human Rights
ECOSOC	Economic and Social Committee
EEZ	Exclusive Economic Zone
EHRR	European Human Rights Reports
EU	European Union
ICC	International Criminal Court
ICCPR	International Covenant on Civil and Political Rights
ICESCR	International Covenant on Economic, Social and Cultural Rights
ICJ	International Court of Justice
ICJ Rep	International Court of Justice Reports
ICLQ	International and Comparative Law Quarterly
ICTR	International Criminal Tribunal for Rwanda
ICTY	International Criminal Tribunal for Yugoslavia
ILC	International Law Commission
ILM	International Law Materials
ILO	International Labour Organisation
GA	General Assembly (UN)
NGO	Non-Governmental Organisation
OAU	Organisation for African Unity (now known as the African Union)
OECD	Organisation for Economic Co-Operation and Development
OSCE	Organisation for Security and Co-operation in Europe
PCIJ	Permanent Court of International Justice
PIL	Public International Law

RAPPORTEUR	A reporter who is appointed by the UN, normally to look into and report on specific topics
SC	Security Council (UN)
UDHR	Universal Declaration on Human Rights
UK	United Kingdom
UN	United Nations
UNEP	United Nations Environment Programme
UNHCR	United Nations High Commissioner for Refugees
UNHCHR	United Nations High Commissioner for Human Rights
UNTS	United Nations Treaty Series
US	United States of America
WHO	World Health Organisation
WTO	World Trade Organisation

Index

This index has been prepared using Sweet and Maxwell's Legal Taxonomy. Main index entries conform to keywords provided by the Legal Taxonomy except where references to specific documents or non-standard terms (denoted by quotation marks) have been included. These keywords provide a means of identifying similar concepts in other Sweet and Maxwell publications and on-line services to which keywords from the Legal Taxonomy have been applied. Readers may find some differences between terms used in the text and those which appear in the index.